Praise for

THE POWER OF YOUR DREAMS

"Pastor Stephanie Ike Okafor is a voice you can trust when it comes to discerning and deciphering the voice of God! Believe it or not, God desires to speak to all of us, even while we are asleep. She illustrates how we can consecrate our dream state as holy ground! *The Power of Your Dreams* isn't just words on a page; it's a tool every believer needs to receive personal instruction for their destiny!"

—TRAVIS GREENE, pastor, recording artist, and author

"Pastor Stephanie Ike Okafor has the unique and powerful gift of merging the wise counsel of God with practical, actionable advice to transform your life. This book will show you how to optimize the quiet intimacy of sleep to absorb lessons direct from the Lord, which will change your life—and the world. This is an immediate must-read and share."

—NICOLE WALTERS, believer, entrepreneur, and the *New York Times* bestselling author of *Nothing Is Missing*

"Stephanie is a unicorn and she's sharing the magic. These pages give muscle and teeth to a spiritual world with which we cohabitate daily but often ignore as insignificant or qualify as too mysterious. Stephanie practices what she preaches, and I can't wait to see how her steadily earned wisdom will change the world. I've never been so excited to go to sleep!"

—BETHANY JOY LENZ, author of *Dinner for Vampires*

"My good friend Stephanie Ike Okafor's new book brilliantly illuminates the connection between our dreams and God's purpose for our lives. This is a must-read for dreamers and believers everywhere!"

—DeVon Franklin, *New York Times* bestselling author

"Stephanie is a rare and much-needed voice at the intersection of faith and culture. A profound and inspiring book, *The Power of Your Dreams* offers insight into the multiple ways that God communicates to us, even through our dreams. This is a book for such a time as this. Stephanie generously shares her personal testimonies to confirm the power of our dreams. 'Each day is an opportunity for God's will to be lived out. And each night is an opportunity for God's will to be revealed.'"

—Natalie Manuel Lee, media personality and
executive producer

"You will be deeply encouraged and strengthened in your personal relationship with Jesus through the wisdom of Stephanie Ike Okafor. She shares her life with vulnerability and reminds us that we do not walk alone. The call of God on Stephanie's life to speak to the heart of this generation—and her insight into God's Word—is powerful!"

—DawnChere Wilkerson, pastor of VOUS Church

"Many Christians often struggle with hearing and knowing the voice of God. In this book, you will discover keys for unlocking the future through discerning God's voice and interpreting dreams. Stephanie has an incredible ability to take you through steps to becoming acutely aware of what is happening beyond the natural realm. You will gain insight into your spiritual life and learn to listen to what God is saying to help shape and guide you in your Christian walk. This book is a must-read for all believers, because we can all develop this gift God has given us to use."

—ALEX SEELEY, pastor of the Belonging Co Church and author of *Tailor Made* and *The Opposite Life*

THE
POWER OF
YOUR
DREAMS

THE

A GUIDE TO HEARING AND

POWER OF

UNDERSTANDING HOW GOD

YOUR

SPEAKS WHILE YOU SLEEP

DREAMS

STEPHANIE IKE OKAFOR

FOREWORD BY TOURÉ ROBERTS

WaterBrook

Italics in Scripture quotations reflect the author's added emphasis.

Details in some anecdotes and stories have been changed to protect the identities of the persons involved.

Published in the United States by WaterBrook, an imprint of Random House, a division of Penguin Random House LLC.

WATERBROOK and colophon are registered trademarks of Penguin Random House LLC.

Library of Congress Cataloging-in-Publication Data
Names: Ike Okafor, Stephanie, author.
Title. The power of your dreams: a guide to hearing and understanding how God speaks while you sleep / Stephanie Ike Okafor.
Description: First edition. | Colorado Springs: WaterBrook, [2024] |
Includes bibliographical references.
Identifiers: LCCN 2024000565 | ISBN 9780593445617 (hardcover; acid-free paper) | ISBN 9780593445631 (ebook)
Subjects: LCSH: Dreams—Religious aspects—Christianity.
Classification: LCC BR115.D74 I44 2024 | DDC 248.2/9—dc23/eng/20240226
LC record available at https://lccn.loc.gov/2024000565

Printed in the United States of America on acid-free paper

waterbrookmultnomah.com

4 6 8 9 7 5

FIRST EDITION

Book design by Ralph Fowler

Most WaterBrook books are available at special quantity discounts for bulk purchase for premiums, fundraising, and corporate and educational needs by organizations, churches, and businesses. Special books or book excerpts also can be created to fit specific needs. For details, contact specialmarketscms@penguinrandomhouse.com.

To my baby girl, Ariel Okafor, I dedicate this book. Before I had the honor of meeting your father and holding you in my arms, I heard your name and saw your sweet face in a dream. You are living proof that dreams are a landscape where God speaks.

FOREWORD

In the early hours of a November morning in 2020, something extraordinary happened to me that changed the course of my life forever. It was a moment that not only transformed me as a person but also set me on a path of faith, impact, and fulfillment that I am still living today.

If I were to pinpoint the turning point that led to more than two decades of success and significance beyond my wildest dreams, it would undoubtedly be that fateful morning and the life-altering encounter I had with God—through a dream. As I sit here reflecting and writing this foreword, I am struck by the realization that every significant shift in my life's journey was either foretold or fore-instructed through a dream.

That particular early morning dream was the catalyst for a series of events that propelled me into a life of purpose and meaning. It was a moment of divine intervention that set me on a path I could have never imagined for myself.

If you consider the characters in Scripture, so many were guided and profoundly impacted by dreams. These accounts range from Abraham, the father of faith, to Jacob, who would later become Israel, the namesake of God's covenanted people. There was Joseph, the dreamer who would ultimately become extremely powerful in Egypt. This Joseph would be second only to Pharoah himself and would go on to save multitudes from a devastating, threatening famine.

There was also King Solomon, who through a dream was tested and, once proven faithful, was made to become the wisest and wealthiest person of his time.

There is an overwhelming amount of men and women to whom God revealed things through dreams. In fact, if you were to remove the accounts of dreams and their significance from Scripture, the seminal events that comprise the fundamental truths we stand upon would have never happened. Without dreams, the wise men who honored the birth of Jesus would have exposed His location to Herod who sought to kill Him. If Joseph, the partner of Mary, wasn't enlightened about Mary's immaculate conception through a dream, he would have abandoned her and the union that was ordained to raise the Savior of the world would have been dissolved. There are countless scenarios we can consider that would drastically change our reality if these dream encounters didn't occur. Thankfully, this is not the case. And hopefully the point I am making is clear: Dreams matter, and not just for ancient biblical characters; they matter for you and me today.

I have had the privilege of watching Stephanie Ike Okafor up close for more than a decade. I watched her serve and work her way up to the top ranks within our organization in Los Angeles. I observed Stephanie grow from one who stood in the lobby welcoming guests as they entered our services to standing on our global stage welcoming multitudes of souls into the kingdom. Stephanie's efforts didn't stop there: She went above and beyond by providing her listeners with rich and insightful revelations about the kingdom and the journey they decided to embark upon. Her voice is one of precision and practicality, and millions have been influenced by her ability to communicate deep spiritual truths, translating them into instantly applicable and implementable disciplines. Stephanie presents *the truth,* and I am hard-pressed to find a better communicator or more compelling voice on the subject of dreams.

I am not only immensely proud of Stephanie and excited about this work, but I am also extremely excited for you. I have no question that the book you're holding in your hands, viewing on your device, or perhaps hearing in your ears will be a catalyst of clarity for you, giving you newfound confidence and a clear path to actualizing God's good plans for your life.

In a world that appears increasingly unstable, uncertain, chaotic, and confusing, the silver lining in it all is that God is still in charge and thankfully still speaking through dreams. This means that there is yet a path through the fog and a guiding light through the obscurity. God is neither in the dark nor will He allow His people to walk blindly. We will know the truth, and the truth shall make us free. One of the greatest truth-revealing tools that God affords us is the enlightening and empowering dreams He sends our way. So, without further ado, let's dive in and become proficient in the meaning of dreams and their interpretation. The journey to clarity awaits us.

—Touré Roberts,
bestselling author, entrepreneur,
investor, and founder of ONE

CONTENTS

When I was in the early stages of my pregnancy, expecting to become a first-time mother, the doctors discovered that I had three large fibroids, tumors that were causing me extreme pain. My husband and I were on vacation in Maui when my ob-gyn at the time called to discuss his recommendation, which was to terminate the pregnancy and undergo surgery to remove the fibroids. But we knew we wouldn't terminate the pregnancy and I had been having dreams about my daughter for years, even before meeting her father. Despite the intense pain, I chose to keep my baby, trusting that God would see me through.

On a particularly difficult night when the pain was unbearable and I couldn't find relief, I walked around our hotel room, my face marked with tears, and began to pray. It was a desperate cry for comfort and healing. I was supposed to preach at our church in Los Angeles that Sunday, but I thought about calling my senior pastor to cancel because of what I was going through.

After finding a little relief and falling asleep, I had a dream. In the dream, I had a powerful encounter with the Lord. He handed me a black leather Bible and assured me that no harm would come to my child. He reminded me that He's with me in both good times and tough times. And He encouraged me not to cancel preaching that Sunday.

The black Bible symbolized my holding on to God's promises.

I contemplated what He had promised regarding childbirth and healing, confident that my baby girl would be okay. Trusting God's unwavering word became my anchor that no matter what, He was with me and He would bring healing and a supernatural childbirth experience.

That dream became a turning point for me. The word I received from God became my truth and declaration in the face of any negative report. I witnessed how the Lord turned things around. Although I was still in pain during the trip, mentally my mindset shifted; I knew it was only for a season.

After we returned home to Los Angeles, I woke up prepared to preach that Sunday morning, even if I had to do it sitting down because of the pain. But to my surprise, the pain had lessened. When I stepped onto the stage to preach, all the pain disappeared. It was a miracle. Trusting in Him and holding on to the words from my dream changed everything. It turned my worry about losing the pregnancy into confidence as I eagerly awaited my baby girl's arrival.

That dream was holy ground.

Holy Ground

One of the most significant biblical and historical figures is a man named Moses. The story of his life is intriguing and remarkable. He was purposed by God to set the nation of Israel free from slavery and lead them in the ways of God. God spoke to him as one would a friend.[1] Their relationship was so intimate that when Moses died, God Himself buried him.

Moses's journey with God was ignited by an encounter on Mount Horeb. The Angel of the Lord appeared to him from within a burning bush that somehow wasn't consumed by the fire. Moses decided to investigate the phenomenon. From the bush, God called to Moses by name. Moses responded, and God instructed him to remove his sandals, for the ground where he stood was holy.

Horeb is a Hebrew word meaning "desolate."[2] It seems ironic that in God's wisdom, He chose a desolate place—a place defined as barren and empty—as the place to make Himself, the creator and giver of life, known to Moses. However, God is the one who fills all things, and so a desolate place by our standards can become a hidden opportunity for an encounter with God.

Mount Horeb wasn't a desolate place. In fact, it was filled with the presence of God. Through this burning bush experience, God called Moses into the awareness that this place was actually holy ground. It was at Mount Horeb that God revealed Himself to Moses as the one true God. It was there that Moses discovered God's wisdom, strategy, and guidance for his purpose as a deliverer to bring the Israelites out of bondage. This location later marked the spot for several life-changing encounters that Moses would have with God.

Dreams are often considered desolate places, seemingly insignificant. But God calls us to holy-ground experiences in our dreams. Through our discovery of God's voice while we sleep, God can reveal His plans for our lives, show what we're purposed to do on earth, give us strategy for breakthrough, and so much more.

Everyone Can Have a Holy-Ground Experience

Upon creating the world, God declared everything He had made "good," but when it came to Adam being alone, He said it was "not good." This inspired the need for the woman to be revealed because she represented the fullness of God's plan regarding the establishment of humankind. This leads us to the first biblical record of sleep.

In the Garden of Eden, "God caused a deep sleep to fall on Adam, and he slept; and He [God] took one of his [Adam's] ribs, and closed up the flesh in its place. Then the rib which the LORD God had taken from man He made into a woman, and He brought her to the man."[3] When God put man to sleep, He was creating both what would benefit man and what would release the intention and purpose of God for humankind.

Sleep is extremely beneficial to our lives. We know getting a full night's sleep can enhance concentration and productivity, improve memory, strengthen the heart, support a healthy immune system, and much more. Moreover, not getting enough sleep can be detrimental to our health: It weakens the immune system, leads to weight gain, and may increase the risk of certain cancers, diabetes, and other health problems. But this isn't simply science stating the health benefits of sleep; it is part of God's design. It's not just about what our bodies need; it's about why God created our bodies to require sleep at all.[4]

The average individual sleeps for twenty-six years of their life,[5] which is equivalent to about one-third of our life span. Why would God create us in a way in which sleep takes up such a huge portion of our lives? If sleep has only natural or physical benefits, does it then take us away from His presence? The answers to these questions can be explored in Adam's experience, and what we find is that while he slept, he was still in God's presence. Sleep simply presented an opportunity for God to reveal His plans and purposes. God, being all powerful, had an infinite number of ways He could have revealed Eve, but He chose to work through Adam's sleep state.

One of many benefits of sleep is that it reminds us that God is ever-present. He is with us at all times—awake or asleep. As you journey through this book, I hope you'll begin to recognize that your dreams are truly holy ground and that they reveal God's wisdom, guidance, and strategy for your life.

Before You Continue

I wrote this book not merely to inform but to equip you to better hear God's voice in your dreams. Here are a few tips to get the most out of this experience:

1. **PRAY:** Take a moment to pray and invite the Holy Spirit to open your heart and deepen your understanding as you start this journey.

2. **ENGAGE:** Each chapter concludes with reflection questions. Resist the urge to skim through them, and instead, embrace the invitation for intentional reflection as you answer these questions thoughtfully.

3. **JOURNAL:** Keep a journal close by to jot down personal notes, respond to reflection questions, and record your dreams, along with any insights into their meanings. This will serve as a valuable tool for tracking your growth, strengthening your memory, and helping you interpret your dreams. Your journal is meant to be a record of your spiritual journey, so use it to capture the evolving landscape of your understanding.

PART I

Hello Dreamer,

I wrote this book with you in mind. The power of dreams is undeniable, but unlocking that power begins with discovering the power of you. You possess infinite possibilities, having been created in the image of the one true, eternal God. For this reason, the first part of this book is dedicated to laying a solid foundation that will equip you with the necessary tools and insights to tap into the full potential of your dreams. By exploring the role you play in receiving and interpreting divine messages from God through your dreams, my goal is to awaken the dreamer in you.

While it's true that I had a natural inclination toward dreaming from a young age, the consistency, intensity, and clarity of these dreams have been enhanced through these insights. I have witnessed remarkable results as people I've mentored have been empowered to have prophetic dreams they never thought possible. Time and again, individuals from all backgrounds have reported how learning to listen for God's voice in their dreams has led to greater clarity about their life and helped them make key decisions with newfound confidence. Such incredible stories serve as a testament to the transformative power of these teachings.

I'm thrilled to be here with you, and I have great expectations of what God will do in and through you as we embark on this journey.

Yours truly,
Stephanie

ONE

GOD SPEAKS TO YOU

In the beginning was the Word, and the Word
was with God, and the Word was God.

—John 1:1

Daring my teenage years, God spoke to me so intensely
that I questioned whether I was truly hearing His voice.
Everywhere I went, I heard Him speak. He spoke to me
about the people around me—friends and family and strangers
He prompted me to pray for, talk to, or encourage. Regardless of
the positive impact those conversations had on people, I wres-
tled with the idea that maybe it was coincidence rather than God.
I wondered, *Is this really the voice of God? Does He always have
something to say?*

At one point, the church I attended hosted a youth retreat
with a guest minister, the late prophet E'vann Walker. My friends
and I were excited for the retreat—but for the wrong reasons.
We hoped to spend time together and with the boys we had
crushes on. Despite all the distractions, that retreat had one of
the greatest impacts on my life.

The retreat opened with a worship night. There were over fifty of us seated on the floor in a conference room. When the minister began to worship, he looked at me and said, "Get up!" I looked around, wondering if he was speaking to someone else. Then he said, "You! I'm looking at you. Get up!" As I got up, he continued, "God wants you to know that He speaks to you. The voice you've been questioning is God speaking to you. It's the same voice you've known for most of your life. You don't need to doubt it. You just need to know Him."

As he was speaking, I felt a power come over me like an electric shock that knocked me to the floor. I missed the rest of the message, and my friends had to fill me in later, but I wasn't harmed, because the power that came over me was the power of God, confirming the message.

In the following days, I pondered that message, especially the words, "You don't need to doubt it. You just need to know Him."

"To know Him" is a weighty statement. It has many layers. For one, there will never be enough time to fully know God. He is the beginning of all things, yet He is not bound to a beginning or an end. He just is. To know Him is the journey of our eternal life.

> God desires to lead you into truth. He speaks, and He speaks *to you.*

Knowing God is to study what He embodies. John 1:1 describes Him as "the Word." Everything created was made through God. Another way to say that is, all things were made through the Word. According to A. W. Tozer, "A word is a medium by which thoughts are expressed."[1] Hence, creation is an expression of God's thoughts; creation speaks of Him.[2] In God's true essence, He speaks. He speaks through creation, He speaks through His Holy Spirit, and He is forever speaking.

Throughout the Bible, we see that God speaks in many ways. Although the Bible is the foundation for knowing His voice, it doesn't limit His communication to you. Concerning the Holy Spirit, Jesus said, "He will guide you into all truth."[3] God desires to lead you into truth. He speaks, and He speaks *to you.*

God speaks to us in various ways, and although dreams are one of those channels, I first want to lay the foundation by examining the four primary ways we experience God's voice: feeling, knowing, hearing, and seeing. In a similar way to how our five physical senses allow us to experience humankind and the world around us, our spiritual senses allow us to experience God's voice. When it comes to these senses, it's common to feel a stronger connection to one over the others. Some people might identify as "feelers" more than "seers." Yet, if you were to consider your physical senses, you wouldn't say you're more of a taster than a toucher, right? You're aware of your ability to use both. Likewise, we have access to each of these spiritual senses; we just need to learn how to tap into them.

Humankind was created in the likeness of God. In Genesis 1:26—a passage from the creation account—God said, "Let us make man in our image, after our likeness" (ESV). How we experience God's voice and receive His word is also a reflection of bearing His image. We have the ability to see like He sees, to feel like He feels, to know like He knows, and to hear like He hears.

So let's dive into a better understanding of these senses, because it's pivotal for us to recognize the richness in the diversity of our spiritual senses and their connection to what happens when we dream.

Four Ways to Experience God's Voice

The Feeler

Feelers are those with a heightened sensitivity to the emotions of God that are connected to our decisions, goals, ideas, plans, and environments. Reading this statement, you might wonder, *Does God have emotions?* John 3:16 is an anchor to our faith, and it says, "For God so loved the world that He gave His only begotten Son." The key word to highlight in the context of emotions is *love.* Because of God's love for humanity, He gave us Jesus. The Scriptures are filled with different expressions of God's emotions. We read of anger,[4] compassion,[5] hate,[6] joy,[7] and much more. Nevertheless, it's important to note that God's emotions are all rooted in His love for humankind and that He never acts unjustly or makes mistakes.

So how do we experience His guidance through our emotions? You might've heard the saying, "I don't feel peace about this." Maybe you've said it yourself when something looks perfect on paper, yet there is an unrest in your spirit. Though you may not understand the sensation, it represents a sensitivity to God's emotions nudging you to recognize that not all that glitters is gold.

In a similar way, there are decisions that seem ridiculous to make, and yet there's a peace you can't explain that reassures you everything will work out. That feeling is an expression of God's voice directing you to move toward that path.

Philippians 4:7 says, "And the peace of God, which transcends all understanding, will guard your hearts and your minds in Christ Jesus" (NIV). In other words, the peace of God doesn't negate what you may be experiencing, but it transcends the natural perception of the situation and communicates His leading.

Peace is the feeling of calmness, which can quiet negative emotions like anxiety, anger, stress, and frustration. It's a directional emotion that speaks to the safety and security of God's guidance in our lives. The *absence* of His peace, however, could speak to being misaligned with your purpose. It could be a signal for you to pause on proceeding with a life-altering decision and to seek Him for clarity.

But notice there's a difference between peace from God and the peace that comes from the world. According to John 14:27, Jesus says, "Peace I leave with you, My peace I give to you; not as the world gives do I give to you. Let not your heart be troubled, neither let it be afraid." Although Jesus reveals the extension of His peace, it is still followed by the command to not be afraid. Regardless of the manner we experience God's voice, it doesn't compel us. We still must make the decision to embrace and live by it.

This gives us a clue for how to discern between God's peace and false peace. False peace isn't the presence of calmness but the drive to quiet our fears instead of following our faith. Although we may be emotionally troubled about making a fear-based decision, we'd rather hold on to what brings us perceived comfort or instant gratification.

Scripture tells of "the rich young ruler," who lived an honorable life, but there was something missing, and it propelled him to inquire of Jesus, "Good Teacher, what shall I do that I may inherit eternal life?"[8] Jesus instructed him to "go and sell all you possess and give to the poor, and you will have treasure in heaven; and come, follow Me."[9] Jesus wasn't seeking for the man to be poor; rather, Jesus discerned that the man's finances were his safety, he identified himself by them, and they would always pose a threat and be a barrier to submitting to God's leading because he valued financial security above everything else. Scripture implies that this man chose to hold on to his riches despite being "deeply dismayed" and "grieving" about his decision.[10] The man's dilemma brought much sorrow, yet he allowed his fears of discomfort and insecurity to drive his decisions.

The peace that comes from Jesus is different. It's not always about the absence of difficulty, because a difficult situation can reveal God's purpose; hardship can reveal what God intends for you. The peace of God is anchored in truth. That's why David said in Psalm 23:4, "Though I walk through the valley of the shadow of death, I will fear no evil; for You are with me." The shadow of death speaks to things that are within proximity of death like disappointments, betrayals, denials, delays, sickness, loneliness, and so on. Yet in the heat of it all, David recognized that because Jesus, the Prince of Peace,[11] was with him, he would make it through.

In embracing the peace of God, there are foundational truths you must know to change your perspective of difficulty.

- First, regardless of your mistakes, you are loved by God.[12]

- Second, God is for you.[13]

- Third, the circumstance is not working against you; it's working for you.[14]

The Knower

You may be a knower if you have an instinctive understanding of what you ought to do and are confident in the decision. This unshakable confidence is rooted in the faith that comes from the Spirit of God[15] to empower you to take a stand, fight for, or move in the direction of God's purpose for your life.

One example of this understanding is when Jesus met two brothers, Peter and Andrew, who were fishermen. While they were fishing, Jesus approached them and said, "Follow Me, and I will make you fishers of men."[16] Even without proof of the full extent of Jesus's identity, they instinctively knew to abandon their nets and follow Him. In the same way, we can possess an unshakable confidence that propels us in a direction that manifests God's will for our lives.

I recall a time in 2021 when a pastor friend of mine was hosting a conference in Nashville, Tennessee, and instinctively I knew I needed to be there. I texted her that I would be attending the conference, and I was looking forward to seeing her. While getting ready to purchase my flight and hotel, I received a message from her about a sudden change. Although this conference had been planned and confirmed a year in advance, one of the speakers could no longer make it due to a family need. Being that I'd already planned to come, my friend asked me if I would speak. Immediately, I knew this was connected to the knowing I felt about my being at the conference. I was grateful that I had been obedient to the word of God through my *inner-knower* because so many lives were blessed. People were supernaturally healed and hope was restored. It was indeed a beautiful move of God's power that took place throughout the entire conference.

Through your inner-knower, you can also have knowledge of things you wouldn't normally be able to because God shares part of His unlimited knowledge with you. For example, at the close of a church service at One Church, I saw a certain man and knew I needed to pray with him and tell him not to be afraid, no matter what he was going through, because God was with him. After I prayed with the man, one of our church staff walked up to me and asked, "Were you just talking to *Black Panther*'s Chadwick Boseman?"

I knew he attended our church, but at the time I didn't recognize him because he'd gone through a drastic weight loss. Later, I began to wonder why the message to him was about not being afraid, and also noticed that simultaneously when I shared it, I felt a sense of loss (the *feeler* in me at work).

A couple of months later when many, including myself, grieved his passing, it was revealed that the cause of death was colon cancer. He'd been battling it for four years, but the information was never made public until he passed. I reflected on our exchange and was reminded that God's presence doesn't mean everything in your life is going great. But He is with you through life's hardest moments to comfort and guide you through.

Some things in life are beyond our understanding, but God uses them to serve a purpose for our good and the good of those connected to our lives. Though you may not see the why or the good outcomes in your lifetime, your difficult moments can become seeds for the next generation.

When I learned about Chadwick's diagnosis, it planted a seed in my heart—and in the hearts of millions of others, I would imagine—to never quit, no matter life's challenges. The diagnosis didn't stop him from being one of the greatest actors. In fact, through it, he became one of the most influential human beings. Could it be that as I was praying with him, he was reminded that he is still loved by God and, regardless of the diagnosis, God is with him? The purpose for that prayerful moment, I may never know in my lifetime, but I am forever grateful for it. It reminded me that when our inner-knower kicks in, it's to serve God's purpose—not our own.

The inner-knower can also be experienced as a memory. Some may refer to this as a déjà vu moment. *Déjà vu* describes an uncanny knowing that you've experienced something when you never have. This often leaves many with unanswered questions about whether it speaks to a past life, or what indeed it is.

Déjà vu experiences communicate through your inner-knower that you are exactly where you need to be, not just regarding the activity you were doing when it happened, but that your season of life is in alignment with God's purpose. Sometimes we get caught up on the hamster wheel of achieving bigger and better, disconnected from the present because it doesn't seem to be glamorous in comparison to the lives of others. We feel unsettled and unhappy about life because ours seems ordinary. Some of us wonder what's fancy or glamorous about being at home all day with the children, working a temp job, being a waitress, serving in the background, volunteering, or helping to raise our siblings. Déjà vu moments can often happen as a reminder that the memory we have right now is tied to the life God already knew about us before time, and we are right where we need to be.

In Psalm 139:16, David shared a revelation about God as it related to his life. He said, "Your eyes saw my unformed body; all the days ordained for me were written in your book before one of them came to be" (NIV). In other words, he was saying, "Before I was formed You knew me, and there's a purpose for each waking day of my life that was already established before I experienced them." Although there's no biblical mention of a déjà vu experience, I believe it speaks to the all-knowing nature of God.

He knew you before you existed, and your mind is simply experiencing what God knows, as He, who is eternal, knew these moments of your life would happen. It's not about a past life but a known one.

However, though these déjà vu experiences can serve as reminders or as confirmation that you're on the right path, they are not to be solely relied on. If you've never had one, don't start questioning your life; this is merely one of the diverse ways we might experience God's voice.

The Hearer

Hearing God's voice is often limited to the idea of hearing His audible voice, which causes many to rule out the experience because it seems out of reach or intimidating. A gentleman once said to me, "I don't think God wants to talk to me. There are billions of people in the world. Why would He take time out to speak to me? That's a lot of pressure." But we underestimate God's love, His desire to speak to us, and the various ways He does.

The hearer experiences God through a voice. This can be outwardly, as an audible voice, or inwardly through an inner voice.

Samuel was called by God to be a prophet to the nation of Israel.[17] A prophet is a spiritual leader who counsels the people of a region and those in authority about the revealed plans and purposes of God.[18]

Through the Holy Spirit, we can prophesy,[19] which is to speak forth the plans of God as they are revealed to us by God. But the difference between being a prophet (the office) and being prophetic is a matter of assignment. Prophets are assigned to regions; they have a burden and a responsibility for territories and their people. Being prophetic refers to the ability to edify, encourage, and equip yourself and those connected to you with spiritual insight for God's purpose.[20] It's important to make this distinction as we learn about Samuel, because although Samuel was a prophet, every aspect of accessing the word of God, including being *the hearer,* is available to all. We just have different assignments.

Samuel, as a young boy, experienced the audible voice of God but initially misunderstood it as Eli's voice.[21] After Eli realized that it was God who was speaking to Samuel, he instructed the boy on how to respond. Notice that Samuel wasn't hearing a strange or frightening voice; it sounded so familiar that Samuel confused it with someone he knew well.

Being that God is the origin of all things, He can speak every language. He can speak to you in a manner that sounds familiar to you or gets your attention. For instance, there was a day that was particularly challenging for me. A couple of things happened in a manner I didn't expect, and in my frustration, I started questioning God, asking, "Where were You? Why did You let this happen?" Although I was asking these questions, I didn't want to hear a response. I just wanted to vent. I concluded that God had abandoned me. Suddenly, I heard a voice say a word that I don't remember now and at the time I had never heard before, and it captured my attention. I paused to look up its meaning and, to my surprise, it was a language that I neither spoke nor understood, and it translated to "listen." God was trying to get my attention to give me the right perspective, but I was so engulfed in my frustration that the moment could only be disrupted by an unusual occurrence.

When my older brother's wife was pregnant with their first child, my brother had an experience where he audibly heard a voice say, "The boy is coming." A couple of weeks later, he and his wife found out they were having a boy. This experience marked my brother's life in such a powerful way. He began to understand that for God to announce the coming of his son before his arrival meant that our lives didn't begin here. Understanding this gave him confidence about the uncertainties of the future.

Hearing God's audible voice isn't as prevalent today as it was in Old Testament times. Prior to the crucifixion and resurrection of Christ, the Holy Spirit wasn't released to dwell within God's people. He was upon them but not within them.[22] When He dwells upon you, your natural senses are the more dominant way to experience God's voice.

When Jesus was baptized, after the Holy Spirit rested upon Him, Matthew 3:17 recounts, "A voice came from heaven, saying, 'This is My beloved Son, in whom I am well pleased.'" Immediately after the Holy Spirit came upon Jesus, the audible voice of God was heard by all who were within proximity. There was a connection between the Spirit coming upon Him and the audible voice being heard.

When the Holy Spirit dwells *within* us, our spiritual senses are more sensitive to serve as a channel to experience God's voice inwardly. You might be familiar with the saying "a voice in my head." There's a beautiful aspect to being able to hear God's voice through our thoughts. Inwardly, God's voice often shows up as a distinctive thought (or series of thoughts)—not alarming but still quite different from our own. His voice in our mind informs, directs, or instructs us, without putting us in perceived harm or danger. That's important to know because it prevents us from confusing His voice with the destructive self-talk that's often triggered by pain or fear.

When I lived with my brother, there was a day we got into a heated argument. I believed he was in the wrong, and I felt justified to dwell in anger. However, when he left the apartment, a distinct and disruptive thought came to my mind: "Go and make your brother's bed." I love making my bed, and though my brother enjoys a made bed, he does not like doing it. This is how I knew there was no possible way the suggestion to make his bed came from me.

Reluctantly, I obeyed the instruction, and I was so thrilled I did, because as I made his bed, I was overwhelmed with love for him. I was no longer upset, and when he returned to the apartment and walked into his room, he saw my act of love as a response to a misunderstanding. He apologized, and we were able to laugh over it without holding on to offense or bitterness. My experience of hearing the voice of God inwardly to make my brother's bed was God's way of communicating to me to let go of the offense and express love to my brother. No matter how we experience God's voice, it will always serve an outcome that draws us closer to the nature and will of God.

When Jesus was preparing the disciples with teachings on how to navigate persecution, He said to them, "But when they deliver you up, do not worry about how or what you should speak. For it will be given to you in that hour what you should speak; for it is not you who speak, but the Spirit of your Father who speaks *in you*."[23] Jesus painted the picture of how God's Spirit spoke inwardly to the disciples, giving them the wisdom and information for what to say in circumstances that went beyond their knowledge or exposure. In the same manner, the Holy Spirit can inwardly speak to us to inform, instruct, and direct us.

In God's sovereignty, we can hear His voice both audibly and inwardly. Neither should be ruled out. But in either case, experiencing God's voice as a hearer shouldn't be feared or doubted as a sign of a mental health disorder. A disorder impairs daily functioning, while experiencing God's voice amplifies it. We don't lose our ability to connect, communicate, and engage in society. On the flip side, we become more compassionate, understanding, confident, caring, relatable, loving, and purpose driven.

The Seer

Our natural sight perceives up to 80 percent of all our sensory impressions, and for this reason, many scientists regard it as the most important of all our human senses.[24] More than the other senses, the eyes best protect us from danger. But you don't need 20/20 eyesight to be a seer, because seers can experience God's voice through both natural and spiritual eyes.

When God in His infinite wisdom chose to use the apostle John to receive His Word through visions, it resulted in the last book of the Bible—the book of Revelation. The word *revelation* comes from the Greek word *apokalypsis,* which simply means "a disclosure of truth."[25] This book unveils Jesus in such a compelling way. It was written because John experienced God's voice as a seer. God instructed him, "What you *see,* write in a book."[26] In my experience and study, the seeing realm is not of sole importance, but it's the most important.

Natural Sight

What an individual sees in the natural is not all there is. There are angelic beings and supernatural activity hidden from our natural eyes. But there are times when God chooses to open our eyes so we can see how the supernatural world partners with the natural world.

My first supernatural experience was in seeing something others couldn't. It was an encounter with an angel when I was nine years old. I still remember the details of that moment as though it happened just five minutes ago.

I grew up in Nigeria in a single-parent household. My father was murdered when I was eight months old. At the time in Nigeria, the justice systems and structure of the economy weren't designed for women to thrive, especially as single mothers. Nevertheless, my mother, my superhero, is a resilient, disciplined, go-getter woman who doesn't take no for an answer. Her life has been an example to me that there's always a way when you're determined to get results. But despite her tenacity, there were still the in-between moments of uncertainty, fear, and doubt.

Before my father was murdered, he was a very wealthy man, but after his death, his older brother demanded everything from us to the extent of sending death threats to my mother, who was now left with three young kids, myself the youngest.

Fighting for justice in a society that wasn't structured to provide it wasn't worth it to my mother to risk leaving her kids as orphans, so she gave over all she had. My mother became an entrepreneur—some days were good and other days brought about uncertainty.

On one of those uncertain days, my mother told us about an

important document she'd been looking for. I remember asking God—who I wasn't sure existed—to help my mother. I wondered and questioned why my father had to die, because if he was still alive, the burden wouldn't be on my mother. Randomly throughout that day, I kept finding old photos of my father in places I hadn't seen before. That night in my bedroom, I found another photo of my father. Suddenly, I sensed a strong presence in my room. I couldn't see the person, but I knew someone was there and I could tell where they were standing.

In my heart, I was at peace, but in my mind, I was troubled because I remembered the scary movies I'd seen. I immediately ran to my mother, who was still awake at the time. The moment I lay down in her bed and before I could share my experience with her, she fell into a deep sleep. Then I sensed the same presence from my room also in my mother's room. I immediately covered my eyes with the blanket. Yet even with my eyes closed I could see a person whose skin seemed to be made of light. I opened my eyes, and I saw the same person. He sat calmly in the middle of the room.

For some reason, in that moment I said within myself, "God, if this is of you, cause wind to flow through my ankles." To date, I believe those words were inspired by the Holy Spirit because there was no way I would've thought to utter that. Within seconds, there was a gush of wind that went *through* my ankles and immediately I was not afraid.

The man stood from his seated position, walked toward my mother, and placed something in her hands. Shortly after, my mother woke up and I told her all that happened. She initially didn't take it seriously, but later in the morning a pastor called her and said, "There was an angelic visitation that took place in your home last night."

To be honest, I needed that confirmation as much as my mother did. Then, later that day, my mother randomly found a document that had some of the information she was looking for. Immediately, I knew that document was connected to the paper that was placed in her hand. I later understood that God had heard us calling for help and spoke to me through the seeing realm.

Psalm 103:20 says, "Bless the LORD, O you his angels, you mighty ones who do his word, obeying the voice of his word!" (ESV). Angels are part of God's kingdom strategy to carry out His plans, which is oftentimes connected to bringing assistance to humanity. For instance, when a prophet named Elisha faced threats and an army was sent against him, he wasn't afraid, but one of his staff was naturally panicked. Elisha prayed, saying, "'LORD, I pray, *open his eyes* that he may see.' Then the LORD opened the eyes of the young man, and he saw. And behold, the mountain was full of horses and chariots of fire all around Elisha."[27]

Elisha knew God had sent assistance in a time of trouble. Experiencing angels through your natural sight should prompt you to be confident in God, not in the angels, because they do His bidding. And know that if you've never seen an angel, it doesn't mean they're not with you. Hebrews 13:2 reminds us that many of us have met angels under the guise of strangers who looked and sounded like us.

Since the seer can see in the natural what others may not see, it's possible for them to also see the dark side of what others don't see—the activities of the demonic. But it's important to understand that when you're submitted to the Holy Spirit, your ability to see is governed by God's will, so no matter what's revealed to you, it cannot harm you and it serves a purpose for your good.

Spiritual Sight

Spiritual sight can be experienced through visions or dreams. Visions can be a download of visual information received through your spiritual sight. Nearly the entire book of Revelation was a vision John received.

Often when I'm praying, God gives me visions that provide profound insight into the subject of my prayers. For example, I remember praying over a project that God had put on my heart to do, but there were other work-related activities that were demanding my time. So I wasn't putting as much effort toward this project as I should have. On a certain day, while I was in prayer for the project, God gave me a vision of an hourglass turned over, with a little bit of sand left to spill into the bottom chamber. In the vision, I heard, "You're running out of time." I immediately understood that what God required from me was better time management to finish what He inspired me to start.

Visions and dreams reveal God's word to us. In the Old Testament, they were a primary way God spoke to people—so much so that when God was quiet, for one reason or another, there was a lack of spiritual sight.[28] Today, visions are still pivotal to experiencing God's voice. They can sometimes be interactive; while being awake, you may be visually and mentally engaged in a supernatural experience with the Lord. The New Testament also gives examples of interactive visions. Acts 9:10 recounts, "Now there was a disciple at Damascus named Ananias. The Lord said to him in a *vision*, 'Ananias.' And he said, 'Here I am, Lord'" (ESV). Then God gave instruction to Ananias on how to carry out God's purpose.

The key difference between visions and dreams is that a vision is given when a person is awake, while a dream, a "vision of the night," is given when a person is asleep.

Dreams Are Unique

Dreams are unique in that we can know, hear, feel, and see all together, and during the restful state of sleep, we are most receptive to experiencing God's voice. Because today the Holy Spirit is with us and in us, God speaks to us in our dreams far more often than we might realize—and it's exciting to harness this. The dream realm provides the opportunity for the rationalism and busyness of humankind to not get in the way. According to Job 33:14–16:

> For God may speak in one way, or in another, *yet man* does not perceive it. In a dream, in a vision of the night, when deep sleep falls upon men, while slumbering on their beds, then He opens the ears of men, and seals their instruction.

The dream realm provides the opportunity for the intelligence and busyness of humankind to not get in the way.

Could it be that while we are doing life, our ears are closed because of the busyness of our days? While we are aware of our daily activities, are we unaware of the voice of God? Our distracted lifestyles cloud the sensitivity required to experience God's voice. So the dream realm becomes a great opportunity for God to instruct us.

In that realm, God can teach us without our "rational" minds interrupting. There's less human argument to counter God's wisdom and instruction, allowing a clearer flow of revelation. Dreams present the best opportunity for you to experience God's voice without being frightened or anxious. Through dreams, God encounters you in your rested state to give you guidance and strategy for your life.

Reflection Questions

1. Reflect on the times you've experienced God's voice in your life. Which of the four ways—feeling, knowing, hearing, or seeing—have you most experienced? Which one would you like to grow in?

2. God speaks to us to communicate and strengthen His relationship with us. Consider what motive is driving you to grow your understanding of your dreams.

TWO

YOU THE DREAMER

Give us this day our daily bread.

—Matthew 6:11

The day I discovered I was pregnant, I screamed in joy. My husband and I weren't planning for it—we'd only been married four months—but we were open to God's timing. Whenever it happened, we had decided, we would embrace it and adjust our lives accordingly.

That day changed everything. I instantly went into mom mode and embraced it. For example, I knew I needed to tailor my nutrition for growing a child. Even though one of my favorite things to eat is sushi, sushi is a no-no for pregnant women.

What a difference one day can make when that day holds revelation and insight. If I hadn't taken that pregnancy test, that day would have been routine. But my ignorance of being pregnant wouldn't have changed the truth of it. On the other hand, gaining the insight that I was pregnant afforded me the opportunity to partner with the truth and take better care of the gift I was carrying.

A Daily Revelation

There's a common saying: "Same thing, different day." Based on our routines and schedules, each day may feel similar to us. The reality is that each one is completely different. What matters is our approach—whether life is happening to us or whether we're proactive about it. This is the power of being diligent with our days. Each day is an opportunity for God's will to be lived out. And each night is an opportunity for God's will to be revealed.

> Each day is an opportunity for God's will to be lived out. And each night is an opportunity for God's will to be revealed.

Jesus emphasized this truth by teaching His disciples to pray for daily bread, as a reference to daily communication with God.[1] In fact, Jesus often likened food to doing God's will, saying, "My food is to do the will of Him who sent Me."[2] Each day holds a distinct revelation to inform our interactions and decisions, and we should seek God's messages regularly in every way that He speaks. Dreams are a powerful means of divine communication, and through them, we have a daily opportunity to receive divine guidance.

A Priceless Treasure

Everyone dreams about two hours each night.[3] Even people born blind can dream with visual imagery.[4] Researchers have discovered we usually have several dreams per night that last from five to twenty minutes.[5] That's a lot of time to receive messages from God! You could have a dream that lasts seven minutes but feels like an entire day. This is one way dreams echo the spiritual realm; when your spirit encounters God in a dream, you don't experience time the same way you do in your waking life, similarly to how 2 Peter 3:8 says that "with the Lord one day is as a thousand years, and a thousand years as one day." The key words there are "with the Lord."

So, if it's proven that everyone dreams, why do some people say they never dream? According to research, about 95 percent of all dreams are quickly forgotten shortly after waking.[6] In other words, everyone dreams, but not everyone remembers. This shouldn't be treated lightly. If you're forgetting a dream that came from God, that's like walking away from a priceless treasure that could transform your life, your family, and the community or world around you.

We see this throughout history—the way dreams have shaped and impacted lives and cultures for generations. Let's examine the stories of a few.

First, we see that our own Messiah's life hung in the balance of a dream. After Jesus's birth, King Herod heard about a child born who was to be "King of the Jews,"[7] and this news troubled him greatly. He viewed the baby as a threat to his kingdom and rulership, so he sought to find the child to kill him. Jesus's life was on the line, and the manner in which God in His wisdom chose to warn Jesus's caretaker, Joseph, was through a dream:

> Behold, an angel of the Lord appeared to Joseph in a
> dream, saying, "Arise, take the young Child and His

mother, flee to Egypt, and stay there until I bring you word; for Herod will seek the young Child to destroy Him." When he arose, he took the young Child and His mother by night and departed for Egypt.[8]

God chose to speak to Joseph through a dream instead of a direct encounter, highlighting how important dreams are to God. Now let's look at some other people whose lives changed because of their dreams. These stories open a window into the mysterious and powerful world of dreams.

World-Shaping Dreams

Dreams have inspired incredible inventions. Take the sewing machine, for example, developed in 1845 by Elias Howe. After he faced several failures, a dream changed everything.

> Howe dreamed that he was building a sewing machine for a savage king in a far-off land. The king gave him 24 hours to complete the machine, but in his dream, as in his waking life, he couldn't get it to work. The deadline passed. The king's warriors came to execute him. As he was being marched to his death, he noticed that the spears held by the warriors were all pierced near the point. All at once he realized—*that* was the solution he had been searching for.[9]

Howe's invention transformed the clothing industry. Production significantly increased, and clothing became more affordable. It also transformed his life, taking him from poverty to wealth, as his design became a standard feature for sewing machines, resulting in substantial royalty payments.

In dreams, we can also receive information that improves our professional performance, increasing our success and influence in the career God has called us to. Jack William Nicklaus, for example, is an American professional golfer known to be one of the greatest golfers of all time.[10] In 1964, he shared with a reporter how a dream helped his golf swing:

> I was hitting them pretty good in the dream, and all at once I realized I wasn't holding the club the way I've actually been holding it lately. I've been having trouble collapsing my right arm, taking the club head away from the ball, but I was doing it perfectly in my sleep. So when I came to the course yesterday morning, I tried it the way I did in my dream and it worked. I shot a 68 yesterday and a 65 today.[11]

In a widely told account, Albert Einstein, the most influential physicist of the twentieth century, had a dream where he was sledding down a steep hill at an immense speed. As he descended, he approached the speed of light. Eventually, the colors of the world around him began to change. He realized that at such high speeds, the laws of physics as we know them would break down. Through this dream, he found inspiration for his general theory of relativity, which revolutionized our understanding of the universe. Einstein's dream shows us that dreams can lead to transformative discoveries in science and technology.

Even movies and stories that capture the hearts of many can originate through dreams. Take the *Avatar* franchise, which came to director and screenwriter James Cameron in a dream when he was nineteen years old.

> I woke up after dreaming of this kind of bioluminescent forest with these trees that look kind of like fiber-optic lamps and this river that was glowing bioluminescent particles and kind of purple moss on the ground that lit up when you walked on it. And these kinds of lizards that didn't look like much until they took off. And then they turned into these rotating fans, kind of like living Frisbees, and they come down and land on something. It was all in the dream. I woke up super excited and I actually drew it. So I actually have a drawing. It saved us from about 10 lawsuits.[12]

When I first learned that *Avatar*—one of my favorite movies—was inspired by a dream, it reminded me of a dream I had as a child about a song. The song was amazing, and I remember waking up with great excitement about it. I told my older brother, and he was shocked that such a well-put-together song had come from a dream. He inquired further, wanting to make certain it wasn't something I'd heard on the radio. I assured him I'd never heard it, except for this first time in the dream.

A couple of months later, the exact song I heard in the dream was released by a well-known artist. It blew me away! I asked the Lord to show me why He allowed me to have that experience. One of the things I learned was that most ideas have a spiritual source. Ideas can come from God, Satan, or self. The Lord was teaching me at a very young age not to take lightly ideas that come to me. They might just be God-inspired ideas for something He has purposed to do on the earth through music, film, science, or education.

Divine Ideas

Maybe you've experienced something similar, where a brilliant and unique idea came to you through a dream or other means of inspiration, but it never materialized beyond casual conversation. Later, someone you've never met creates the very thing that was once "your" idea, leaving you wondering how it happened. There are two possible explanations—God may have been teaching you about ideas and divine intelligence, or the idea was revealed to you because you had the capacity to produce it, as I have experienced numerous times. Many of the projects I've executed were born from visions or instructions that came through dreams.

However, we don't own these divine ideas; they are merely revealed to us. In the end, God partners with those who are willing to do the work to make the idea a reality. Whatever God has purposed will be established through whoever is willing and surrendered. If you've received such dreams, pay attention to them, and seek confirmation humbly through prayer to determine if it's something God desires to partner with you on.

Here's a simple prayer:

> *Dear heavenly Father, I commit this dream to You. If this vision is something You desire for me to fulfill on earth, please burden my heart with it. Grant me wisdom, understanding, and strategy on the steps I need to take to bring it to fruition. Also, please grant me favor with those who can assist me in executing it,*

and bring divine relationships to aid in its realization.
If I struggle with doubt or feel like giving up, please
make Your presence known to me, and remind me that
You are with me. May I not get blinded by selfish gain,
and if the season arrives that You need me to walk
away from it, may Your will be done. In Jesus's name,
amen.

God's Intention to Speak

God never speaks in vain. His words are always on assignment to bring us into alignment with His will and purpose for our lives. For this reason, He speaks to everyone—believers and unbelievers alike—because we were all created with a purpose. God has a plan for everyone on the earth.

When we begin to recognize we weren't created to be dependent on our wisdom but to become more surrendered to God, we become more sensitive to His voice and leading. Take, for instance, Pilate. After Jesus was betrayed by Judas and taken by the authorities under false accusations, Pilate, who was governor of the Roman province of Judaea and the official who presided over the trial of Jesus, recognized the people's envy concerning Him.[13] Something about Pilate's heart posture wasn't willing to fully rely on public opinion. Rather, he had a desire to search out the truth. It's no coincidence his wife had a dream that confirmed Jesus's innocence: "While he was sitting on the judgment seat, his wife sent to him, saying, 'Have nothing to do with that just Man, for I have suffered many things today in a dream because of Him.'"[14]

Although none of this prevented Jesus's crucifixion, the dream was likely purposed to reveal truth and exempt Pilate and his wife from the guilt of murdering an innocent man. Pilate couldn't stop the accusers' demands, but he did declare Jesus a "just Person," exactly as his wife shared with him.[15] In this incident, God partnered with Pilate and his wife, using their curiosity about the innocence of Jesus to bring them into truth.

Here's how that impacts you. As you become curious about your life, the things connected to you, and what God can do through you, you'll begin to recognize and cherish every day as an opportunity to partner with God through your dreams and be led into truth.

You already dream. That space already exists. The problem is, many don't remember the information that was delivered. To help prevent your dreams from being forgotten, let's dig into some spiritual principles of dreams.

The Block Is Real

Just as we can block a person from our phone, social media, or email, we can set up a spiritual block. Our dreams are a way God communicates with us, and spiritual blockages can keep us from receiving or remembering those dreams. This is because effective communication requires access.

In our relationship with God, the heart is the access point for communication. Notice how the word *ear* is embedded in the word *heart*. It is through the heart that we receive and understand messages from God. When our hearts are pure and free from contaminants, communication with God is easy. Nothing blocks it. This is why Matthew 5:8 says, "Blessed are the pure in heart, for they shall see God." The purity of our hearts gives us access to experiences of God, which include sharing intimacy with Him, receiving instructions, and gaining clarity.

When our hearts are hardened, our ability to receive those communications from God is dulled. Biblically, there is a connection between a person's inability to understand or perceive a message from God and their hardened heart.[16] It's no coincidence that a person with a hardened heart can also be described as "blind."[17] When we forget our dreams, we may have become blind to their messages, despite their importance.

Through my own relationship with God and my experience as a pastor, I've discovered two primary factors that block our communication with the Lord: unforgiveness and fear.

Blocked by Unforgiveness

Growing up without a father, I had a lot of suppressed anger. As a child, I would often fantasize about the death of those involved in my father's murder. It didn't help that most of my friends grew up with both parents. Seeing their families was a constant reminder of what I was robbed of, and my anger and bitterness only grew.

When I encountered God at nine years old, there was a moment He taught me the importance of loving others—including those we deem our enemies. I'll never forget the words He spoke that changed my heart posture. He said, "No one hurts you from a place of love or wisdom." I realized those that hurt us are victims of their own brokenness, which is exploited by the Enemy to carry out his bidding.

Have you ever wondered why Judas committed suicide after betraying Jesus?[18] To give you a context, Judas was one of the twelve disciples who followed Jesus. One of his responsibilities was to oversee the money bag. This means he oversaw the finances regarding Jesus and His followers' food and shelter or for ministry purposes. But Judas also struggled with integrity. We know this because it was recorded that he would steal from the money bag.[19]

Now, Jesus didn't give Judas this role with the money bag by mistake. Rather, He heals what we are willing to reveal. Sometimes He will put us in a position or a circumstance that's intended to show our weakness and our need for His healing.

But Judas was too caught up in the brokenness of his greed to see the truth. Even though Jesus chose Judas to follow Him from a place of love, to heal and restore him so he could come into the fullness of his God-given potential, Judas saw it as an opportunity for selfish gain. That's why, in conversation with those who sought Jesus's life, Judas asked, "What are you willing to give me if I deliver Him [Jesus] to you?"[20] Judas was willing to betray Jesus from a place of his brokenness, and that opened the door for Satan to influence his behavior. After the deed was done, and Judas realized the role he played, the guilt felt too much to bear and he ended his life. His misguided behavior is similar to that of those under the influence of drugs or alcohol and not fully coherent of their actions or the ripple effect of their decisions. Judas was neither drunk nor on drugs, but he was under a different kind of influence: a demonic influence.[21]

I share this story about Judas to remind us that oftentimes when people hurt us and we struggle to forgive—and likely for valid reasons—the truth is that person wasn't the real source that hurt you. Rather, their weakness and brokenness opened a door for the Enemy to influence their behavior against your life. Ephesians 6:12 states, "For we do not wrestle against flesh and blood, but against principalities, against powers, against the rulers of the darkness of this age, against spiritual hosts of wickedness in the heavenly places."

We were created in the image of God. Through our relationship with Jesus, we can walk into the restoration of that image. On the other hand, deceit, manipulation, control, abuse, and toxic patterns are evident in a person who has not discovered their true nature. And that lack of discovery leads to casualties that impact people like you and me. It's also true that *our* brokenness has hurt others as well. It may not be to the same magnitude, but you might be surprised to learn someone holds bitterness and unforgiveness toward you for something you did while "under the influence."

Of course, forgiveness shouldn't be confused with the restoration of a relationship. Real restoration requires a mutual understanding of wrongs and the embrace of healthy change. Neither should forgiveness be confused with an exemption of consequences. Forgiveness is the embrace of our identity in God, which is an identity of love.[22] It guards the purity of our heart. It doesn't necessarily mean the offender will change, but it's a solution to keep the poison out of us.

Unforgiveness poisons our access to true intimacy and fellowship with God because unforgiveness is subtle hate. It develops hate and bitterness in us toward another—emotions that go beyond a feeling into thinking and being. Although it may seem to affect only one area of your life, unforgiveness slowly takes over how you see and interact with people. It creates a layer of negative judgment toward the actions of others and events that occur, all of which can block you from receiving truth. It's a limitation, by default, to the things your heart can receive from God.

Sometimes it might not be what another person did that caused unforgiveness to fester in our hearts. It could be something *we* did—the mistakes we've made. Maybe, like Judas, you've identified yourself as your mistakes. I'm happy to tell you there's an alternate path. Your story doesn't have to end like his. There's nothing you've done that's a shock to God. He is all knowing, and He still chooses you. He still has plans for you. It's time to let go and take hold of purpose and truth. When you walk in purity of heart, you are positioned to walk with God, your sensitivity to His voice is heightened, and you are able to receive His messages. Your communication channels are unclogged.

Blocked by Fear

You may be aware that the most repeated commandment in the Bible is "Do not fear"?[23] Similar to unforgiveness, fear hinders us from walking with God. This is because fear is a barrier to the embrace of God's love. According to 1 John 4:18, "There is no fear in love; but perfect love casts out fear, because fear involves torment. But he who fears has not been made perfect in love."

Let me point out that the kind of fear I'm talking about here is not the fear that is an emotional response to a perceived danger, threat, or harm. That kind of fear is a natural, protective mechanism that helps us navigate and respond to actual danger. The type of fear in 1 John is that which cripples and debilitates our ability to live out our true purpose. It's the kind of fear that corrupts the truth about the love of God, His Word, His promises, and His character. This type of fear draws its power from uncertainty.

When I was growing up, a family member and I were exposed to the supernatural at a young age. We had several experiences that defied logic and natural reasoning. Surprisingly, we responded differently to the encounters we had with God. I embraced them because, for one, I couldn't deny them, and two, I was curious to know more about God. I wanted to understand the biblical experiences I was having, such as seeing angels, having dreams about things before they happened, and so on.

On the other hand, this family member responded with fear. They viewed the experiences through a lens of losing control. If they couldn't logically understand how these experiences happened, they didn't want to engage. Their fear wasn't so much about what they saw as it was about embracing the supernatural.

While my encounters with God and messages from Him amplified, the opposite happened to this family member. The Spirit of God is never forceful, according to Revelation 3:20. Jesus said, "Behold, I stand at the door and knock. If anyone hears My voice and opens the door, I will come in to him and dine with him, and he with Me." When we open the door through our trust, belief, and confidence in the love, wisdom, and leadership of God, He communes with us. Unfortunately, although many have a desire to open the door, the fear of the unknown keeps them from turning the knob.

When you think about the areas in your life where fear caused you to resist taking a step toward something you desired, you most likely experienced some uncertainty about the outcome. This is because fear draws its power from uncertainty.

Uncertainty can be a gift or a curse to your imagination, depending on where you place your confidence. If you place confidence in what you see or can control, then you'll likely have an underlying fear about anything that could disrupt your sense of normalcy. That fear can often block communication from God because the desire to receive messages from God is in fact an invitation for disruption.

I believe every one of us has a natural inclination to settle for less than our true potential, because our expectations are on the level of our experiences and exposure, which always fall short.

Psalm 139:17–18 records, "How precious are your thoughts about me, O God. They cannot be numbered! I can't even count them; they outnumber the grains of sand! And when I wake up, you are still with me!" (NLT). The author of that psalm, David, was a shepherd boy whose life was transformed by the word of God that revealed him to be a king. He never limited the possibilities of what God could do with him. David tapped into a truth about God's thoughts about us, which is that if His thoughts toward us are endless, who must we be? David's life and confidence were never shaped by what he saw, but rather by what God said. What is it that God knows about you that you haven't even scratched the surface of? The curiosity to ask such questions or think in such a manner lives on the other side of your fear.

> The desire to receive messages from God is in fact an invitation for disruption.

In 2020, I taught a message on the interpretation of dreams that garnered over one million online views. Afterward, many people reached out to me about their struggle to remember their dreams. Some believed they simply didn't dream, while others were troubled by knowing they had a dream but couldn't recall the details. I committed some time to one-on-one counseling sessions with a couple of individuals, and fear was a key issue many shared. They feared that a message from God would confirm their need to make a change about something they idolized. This fear blocked them from understanding God's voice in their dreams.

Idols can come in many forms: things, people, a career, a place. They are external elements we cling to for validation, worthiness, meaning, security, and more. When they become idols, the thought of losing them can cripple our sense of identity so subconsciously that we naturally refrain from anything or anyone that could disrupt our false sense of certainty.

Let me give you an example. I shared some pastoral counseling sessions with a young lady I'll call Stacy. Her idol was a toxic relationship. She was dating a guy who was unfaithful to her. When she would bring up conversations about their future, he would manipulate the situation and gaslight her for questioning his commitment. Deep down, Stacy knew this relationship had no true future. They'd been dating on and off for years, and he'd always displayed the same toxic patterns. But she argued that they were in love and that eventually he would change his ways.

As we dug deeper, we discovered Stacy wasn't holding on to that relationship because of love. Prior to meeting him, she had struggled for years with a sense of insecurity and unworthiness. Then came this wealthy and influential man. She loved the moments of feeling wanted by him. It made her feel seen. The relationship gave her a sense of worthiness. But it became an idol in her heart—a way of coping rather than becoming.

Coping might seem like the easy way out, but it keeps you small, never fully discovering the greatness within you or the possibilities that surround you—which always involve some degree of disruption to your thinking and your way of life. The desire to hear from God includes a willingness to relinquish control in order to accept His guidance over your life. God's voice cannot occupy the same space as your idols. To have clarity, only one voice can lead you.

If you've struggled with fear and suspect it's a culprit for why you can't recall your dreams, be encouraged that you have the power to choose hope. Many of us set alarms on our phones to wake us up each morning, yet we have no control over or certainty about whether we'll wake up. We have hope that we will.

Stacy eventually clung to hope. Although she faced uncertainty about love and her desire for marriage and a family, she walked away from false comfort, mourned the loss of what-ifs, and opened her heart to new possibilities. She began to dream again, both literally and figuratively. She learned how to love herself and receive imagery of how God sees her. She truly turned from fear to hope in God.

If fear has been blocking you from remembering your dreams, you can choose hope. Hope is a powerful disruptor because it reminds us that every storm eventually runs out of rain and that present challenges aren't permanent. Hope reminds us of the truth that regardless of life's uncertainties and the challenges we must go through, what's ahead is greater than where we've been. I've discovered we aren't so much afraid of losing. Rather, it's the becoming that really scares us—to be more than we've known, more than our environment has seen, and to go beyond safety and travel the narrow path into destiny.

> You are a child of God. Your playing small does
>   not serve the World.
> There is nothing enlightening about shrinking.[24]

You don't have to play it safe when you know God is with you and His word to you is evidence of His presence and power.[25] As you open up to Him, embracing His love and letting go of the fear, be encouraged that His Word reveals truth, and it reveals you.

Expect and embrace disruption, and you'll discover greatness through dreaming with God.

New Every Morning

Divine dreams can be an expression of God's mercy. They are His compassionate response to our desire for His voice in our lives, for truth, and for the pursuit of the ideas He has placed on our hearts. Even when we don't have words or language for these needs, He hears the cry of our hearts and acknowledges the steps we take toward Him. They might be baby steps, but each one is significant to Him.

As you take a step forward, desiring God to communicate with you through dreams on a regular basis, His mercy allows those baby steps to have a giant impact. According to Lamentations 3:22–23, "The steadfast love of the LORD never ceases; his mercies never come to an end; they are new every morning" (ESV). Every morning you are awakened to hold the treasure of divine direction in your life. Just as the mercies of God are made new every morning, so you have an opportunity to receive from Him through your dreams every morning too. As you reach for that opportunity, pray this prayer:

> *Heavenly Father, I come before You humbled by the thought of Your mercy and goodness. In Your mercy, speak to me. Restore the power of my dreams, that they will be a daily channel of communication with You. Your Word is the source of my strength—may it never depart from me. In Jesus's name, amen.*

Reflection Questions

1. What is the main reason you think you may not always remember your dreams?

2. In learning about how dreams have impacted and shaped lives and cultures, share your hopes for your dreams.

THREE

PREPARE YOUR
BODY AND SOUL

Go, borrow vessels from everywhere,
from all your neighbors—empty vessels;
do not gather just a few.

—2 Kings 4:3

Preparation makes room for partnership. It creates a space for God to fill. So often we expect God to meet us in a space we haven't made ready for Him.

There's a story in 2 Kings 4 about a widow who cried out to the prophet Elisha for help to pay her late husband's debt to protect her two sons from being taken as slaves. In those days, a person's cry to a prophet was a demonstration of their cry to God, because the prophets represented the mouthpiece of God. Surprisingly, Elisha didn't ask the woman how much she needed. Instead, he asked, "What do you have in the house?"[1]

All she had at the time was a small jar of olive oil. Elisha built upon that and told her to ask her neighbors for empty jars, gathering as many as she could. Then he instructed her to take the little jar of oil she had and pour it into the jars she borrowed from her neighbors. Supernaturally, an abundant supply filled every jar, and it stopped flowing only when there was no jar left. Then Elisha instructed her to sell the oil and pay her debts, which would sustain her family.

Her story offers a lot of incredible insights about how God works. The widow first needed to make room for God by having something He could fill. He filled what she had readied. God never lacks in His ability to meet our needs, but we are limited by how much we prepare to receive. The room we provide is the room He fills. The quality of our readiness can expand our capacity for encounters with God in our sleep.

Preparation is vital.

God equips us before sending us. Jesus lived thirty-three years on the earth, and out of that, only three years were carved out for His earthly assignment. Most of those years were spent being equipped. It's important to understand this, because as we prepare to encounter God in our dreams, we must make a change in our discipline, and that doesn't happen overnight. It requires intentionality, time, and consistency. Embrace the need to prepare immediately, but expect results gradually.

> Embrace the need to prepare immediately, but expect results gradually.

There are key disciplines that can help us grow in faith. Remember, it's important to be consistent. We shouldn't get discouraged if we don't see immediate results. This is a process. Whether we experience back-to-back prophetic dreams or seemingly no change at all, we can't give up.

Faith is often proved by consistency. Sometimes God will wait to see our consistency as evidence of our faith. Faith means the difference between something happening and not happening, because our faith joins us to God. It is our agreement with

God that gives us permission to encounter or experience what He has for us. Unbelief, on the other hand, is dangerous because it creates distance between us and God's Word. If we separate from the Word, we are no longer able to produce its intended purpose.

So, how should we prepare?

There are four key areas to focus on as we make room for God to communicate in our dreams—they include our soul, food and rest for our bodies, and what I refer to as the first ninety seconds.

Preparation for Dreams

The Soul's Intake

You were created as a tripartite being, consisting of three parts: spirit, soul, and body. This distinction can be recognized in 1 Thessalonians 5:23, which says, "May God himself, the God of peace, sanctify you through and through. May your whole spirit, soul and body be kept blameless at the coming of our Lord Jesus Christ" (NIV).

When God first created man, He formed him from the dust of the ground, which is the body and flesh. Then He breathed into him "the breath of life,"[2] which is the spirit of the man. And immediately man became a living soul. This suggests to us that when the spirit of man encountered the body, the soul was produced. Although they are intertwined, the spirit and soul function separately. God communicates to your spirit, and it's translated through your soul. The soul determines how you perceive and receive messages from God.[3] That's why when people share messages they received from God, it has various forms of expression and meaning regarding the language or symbols used that could translate as something completely different to someone else.

The soul is the seat of our intellect and emotions (what we commonly think of as our mind and heart), as well as experiences and free will. What you expose your soul to can either bring clarity or contaminate messages from God. It is for this reason that Satan is an enemy of your soul.[4] He cannot touch your spirit, and your earthly body is already destined for death, but if he can influence your soul, he can have victory over your life.

The concept of "the soul's intake" is an important one to understand, as it can significantly impact our overall well-being. What we consume visually, audibly, or experientially—through what we watch, read, listen to, or experience in our daily lives—is all part of the soul's intake. This exposure has the power to influence our thoughts and emotions in either a positive or negative way. As believers, it's essential that we choose our intake wisely, because anything that leaves us inspired, encouraged, and full of faith is good for our soul, while anything that leads us to negative thoughts, emotions, and patterns is bad for the soul.

In Philippians 4:8, Paul advised us to think about things that are true, pure, and praiseworthy. What we let into our minds matters because it shapes how we think and feel. Spending time with God's Word is like giving our minds a healthy meal—it helps us think the way God wants us to. This is also why worship is so transformative: It allows us to set our minds on God, which shifts our focus away from fear and anxiety toward faith and confidence in Him. As Isaiah 26:3 says, "You will keep him in perfect peace, whose mind is stayed on You, because he trusts in You."

Now, here's the connection to dreams. What we let into our

minds and hearts before sleeping can impact the types of dreams we have. Negative or fearful things might lead to nightmares, but positive and faith-filled content creates a better environment for receiving messages from God. Be mindful about what you focus on before bedtime. Instead of horror movies or negative media, try reading the Bible, listening to worship music, or praying. That way, you're preparing yourself to be more sensitive to the Holy Spirit, increasing the chances of having dreams that bring messages and insights from God. We are shaped by what we behold. By beholding the Lord before going to bed, we make room for continued communication through our dreams. However, if the last thing we see is a scary movie, that's what might show up in our dreams. The spirit of fear expressed through film isn't from God; it's a way for Satan to influence your dreams.[5] Being intentional about your soul's intake is important if you want to hear God's voice in your dreams.

Food

In 2018, Burger King created a Halloween sandwich called the Nightmare King that was clinically proven to induce nightmares.[6] They conducted a sleep study over ten nights with one hundred participants and found that eating the Nightmare King increased a person's chances of having nightmares by three and a half times. One of their participants recalled an alien attacking the boat he was on in his dream.

You might wonder how a burger can increase the chance of having a nightmare. According to the study's lead doctor, the burger's combination of cheese and protein led to the vivid dreams. Some might call this a coincidence, but it seems advisable, regardless, to avoid heavy, fatty foods before going to bed if you desire a healthy dream life. It's why people often conclude that a dream was a "pizza dream" due to eating too much pizza or a fatty meal before going to bed.

On another note, research highlights the damaging effects of poor eating habits on cognitive function. Consuming a diet high in saturated fats and sugar can lead to brain fog, impaired memory and cognitive deterioration.[7] These effects can be detrimental to our ability to hear from God through dreams and feel motivated to do as He says. On the contrary, a well-nourished body and mind can lead to improved cognitive function, increased clarity, and sharper focus, preparing us to better tune in to God's voice.

I understand an additional spiritual connection between food and intimacy with God, because how you treat your body has spiritual significance. We read in 1 Corinthians 6:19–20, "Do you not know that your bodies are temples of the Holy Spirit, who is in you, whom you have received from God? You are not your own; you were bought at a price. Therefore *honor God with your bodies*" (NIV). A healthy body can carry out the will and purpose of God. This is one way taking care of your body honors God.

As self-control is a fruit of the Holy Spirit, your ability to exercise self-control is evidence of the Holy Spirit's influence in your life. You are more sensitive to God's messages in your dreams when His Spirit governs you. You don't want to create opportunities for the Enemy to corrupt your dreams through your habits and lifestyle, and this includes the food you put into your body. Instead of sugary snacks before bed, try a light and healthy choice like a banana. In fact, bananas have nutrients that can help you remember your dreams.[8]

Caring for your physical body is essential for fulfilling God's plans and purposes on the earth since your body enables you to engage with the world. The fact that Jesus had to become a human—with a human body—underscores the intrinsic value of our physical bodies. Living a healthy lifestyle is crucial to ensuring that you can carry out God's plans and purposes to the fullest.

Rest

If you've ever, like me, allowed your computer battery to completely run out before reaching for the charger, you've likely noticed it begins to damage your battery. I've learned that letting our computers run to empty shortens the life of the battery, causes data loss, and can corrupt unsaved files.

In the same way, your body isn't at its optimal health if you consistently drain it before going to bed. In these cases, your body is not in a state of rest but exhaustion. You aren't giving your mind the ability to properly and effectively shut down from the busyness of the day. This, too, could cause data corruption—that is, corruption of the information God desires to plant in your spirit through dreams.

According to Ecclesiastes 5:3, "a dream comes through much activity, and a fool's voice is known by his many words." When your mind has been solely focused on a particular problem, task, or person all day, your dreams can be influenced or corrupted by the loudness of your soul. This is why the scripture includes the latter part about recognizing a fool's voice—there's a connection to be drawn. Just as the many words of a fool hold no weight, dreams tainted by the noise within hold no significance. Rest, therefore, becomes crucial. God Himself instituted rest, as seen in His resting on the seventh day after creating the heavens and the earth. This rest was blessed by God, highlighting its importance and value.[9]

If our hope is in our achievements, we will feel stressed when we fail to meet our goals. Our personal lives will take a hit, and rest will feel like a luxury. This is because our hope is not in God but in our abilities and accomplishments. But when we place our hope in God, we realize that our worth and value come from Him. We can find rest in the knowledge that God loves us unconditionally and has a plan for our lives.

Certain messages cannot be heard in a loud atmosphere. God spoke in a still, small voice to the prophet Elijah, which required proximity to the sound of the voice to hear it.[10] When it comes to dreams, that proximity can be gained through the quietness of soul we bring to bed, which allows us to perceive what has been downloaded to our spirit.

Rest includes making sure we get enough hours of sleep each night. But it's more than that. It's about living in a rhythm of rest—resting after work, taking time to quiet our souls, releasing ourselves from the work and worries of the day, being present. This could start in our cars when we're on our way home after a long day. We can maximize that alone time to be in worship and release our day before God.

If you have a family at home, be present with them. Take time to check in with one another, to laugh together, and to love each other. When we are not consumed by the worries each day brings, we practice trust in God that He is in everything, including all the details of our lives. Our interactions with loved ones and our self-talk at the end of the day can reveal where our hope lies. If our hope is in God, we will demonstrate the fruit of His Holy Spirit, such as peace, joy, kindness, gentleness, and love.[11]

These fruits are not seasonal, and regardless of our circumstances or challenges, we can remain confident in God and find rest in the midst of storms. As David said in Psalm 62:5, "My soul, be quiet before God, for from him comes my hope" (ISV).

If it's a struggle for you before sleeping to slow down enough to release the anxieties of the day by prayer and worship, then read Psalm 23 out loud every night before going to bed. Let your mind find rest in its promises. Take time to think about the words as you say them. Allow the peace of God to come upon you and quiet the noise of anxiety, worry, and the burden of responsibility.

When you go to bed in a rested state of mind, you posture yourself in the blessing of God. This gives your soul an opportunity to receive what God desires to communicate to your spirit.

The First Ninety Seconds

Some dreams have a powerful grip on our memory, and no matter how hard we try to forget them, we remember every detail with great precision. These dreams might stay with us for years.

On the other hand, have you ever woken up from a dream and found that you can't remember any of it? It's happened to me before, and I've realized that how I engage the first ninety seconds after I wake up can determine whether I'll remember my dreams or not. It's a small window, but it's critical to what I remember from my dreams. I've found that if I take the time to reflect within the first few seconds of waking, I remember more details of my dream.

Sometimes I've forgotten dreams that I knew were important, and I regretted losing the message from God that was embedded in them. In these cases, I've found that humbling myself through prayer and asking the Holy Spirit to bring the dream back to my memory can help. Alternatively, something throughout my day may trigger the memory of the dream.

Forgotten dreams can still hold valuable messages from God. But if we regularly disengage too quickly and get distracted by our natural environment, we risk losing the messages that God may have intended for us. It's alarming to think how many significant dreams can be forgotten, not because God didn't send a message but because the message was locked in our spirit.

It's vital that your sleeping environment doesn't distract you the minute you wake up. Consider investing in an alarm clock instead of using your phone to avoid the temptation to scroll through emails, text messages, or social media immediately upon waking up. Keep a dream journal and pen at your bedside, with the expectation that you will have a dream.

> Forgotten dreams can still hold valuable messages from God.

When you wake up from a dream, immediately write down all the details that you remember, including what you felt. Later, when we dive into interpreting dreams, you'll discover that details matter, from numbers to people to location, actions, emotional tone, names, and colors. Preserving the details of the dream is essential for understanding and interpreting the dream accurately. At this stage, it's not necessary to analyze where the dream came from (self, Satan, or God). Simply write it down. If you're feeling extremely fatigued, write down abbreviated details that can trigger your memory later to recall the full dream.

The key is to capture as much as you can for the first ninety seconds after you open your eyes, before the soul gets loud and distracted by the demands of the day. By taking this time to remember and preserve the details of your dreams, you open yourself to receiving invaluable messages from God.

Discipline, Discipline, Discipline

One of the key points I've learned in my walk with Christ is that disciples are disciplined. To be a disciple is to be a follower of Jesus, and this means walking with Him and having intimacy with Him. Salvation opens you up to a relationship with Jesus; it welcomes the Holy Spirit to take up residence in you. But to become mature in Christ and build intimacy with Him requires discipline. The writer of Hebrews put it this way: "No discipline seems pleasant at the time, but painful. Later on, however, it produces a harvest of righteousness and peace for those who have been trained by it."[12]

My close friend Roosevelt Stewart II said, "Discipline goes from duty to rhythm to delight then desire." I love that breakdown because it acknowledges that discipline is never fun in the beginning. But it's our duty because certain dimensions in God cannot be accessed until we introduce discipline into our lifestyle. Then it becomes a rhythm. When you consistently practice it, it becomes something you no longer think about doing. You just do. Afterward it's a delight! You start to enjoy it because sowing a habit consistently produces a harvest. You start to enjoy the fruit of it. Finally, it becomes a desire. You recognize your need for it, and you long for it. When you're placed in an environment that throws off your rhythm, your desire for that discipline keeps you intentional.

Discipline is not typically born out of desire, but rather a sense of commitment. So, to have prophetic dreams, you must commit to the practices that prepare you for them. Take notice if you catch yourself thinking, *Do I really have to do all this?* That might be a subtle sign that you don't want to put in the effort, which is a feeling that often comes from unbelief. We can easily get caught up in the surface problems without addressing the root cause. Some people think they're simply lazy or procrastinating when the real issue is unbelief. If you feel like it's all too much, take a break and go back to read the earlier chapters. When you pray, ask the Holy Spirit to show you what's important for you, and build habits around those things.

Preparation requires discipline. By being mindful of our soul intake, the food we consume, our rest, and the first ninety seconds after waking, we set the stage for God to communicate with us through our dreams.

Heavenly Father, I want to understand and remember Your messages in my dreams. Show me how I can prepare myself better to hear from You, and strengthen my desire with discipline. In Jesus's name, amen.

Reflection Questions

1. Which of the four areas for preparation stands out the most to you, and why do you think that is?

2. What are one or two practices you can implement today to begin preparing yourself to better receive God's messages in your dreams?

PART II

Hello Dreamer,

It's time for us to get personal. No two dreamers are the same, so we'll be diving deeper into the unique language of your dreams and unraveling the messages they hold. As we journey together, my desire is for you to develop a personal understanding of your dreams in order to enhance your relationship with God and gain direction for your life.

Your dreams are unique, a personal narrative crafted by God just for you. The dream world is a place where He reveals secret things to us about ourselves, people around us, and our future. It's vital to explore the mystery and significance of your dreams. By doing so, you'll gain greater insight into your life and increase your spiritual understanding. You are uniquely designed, fearfully and wonderfully made, and your dreams offer a glimpse into that design.

I invite you to open up your heart, be willing to learn, and trust that God will guide you through this journey.

Yours truly,
Stephanie

FOUR

THE SOURCE OF DREAMS

Beloved, do not believe every spirit,
but test the spirits, whether they are of God.

—1 John 4:1

"In my dream, God showed me you're my wife!" These were words I never wanted to hear again.

For my first seven years serving as a pastor, I was single in a church that was overflowing with people my age. As a woman in a position of visibility, influence, and authority, I was conscious of the responsibility that comes with the role. Too often, people have been hurt and exploited by pastors and churches that fail to recognize their influence. So, early on, I made a promise to God, a vow that I wouldn't date anyone within my church community, believing that God would connect me to my spouse in a different way—which He did! I chose this path to keep my heart pure and focused on the ministry. This decision ensured that every time I counseled or prayed for someone of the opposite sex in a moment of vulnerability, it remained without confusion. My decision wasn't always popular, and some saw it as extreme, but they also didn't share my experience of multiple eligible men sending me unsolicited emails, conveying messages through third parties, or approaching me with claims that God had revealed to them in their dreams that I was their wife. Either they were all lying, or indeed they had dreams but misinterpreted the source. Dreams can be misleading, especially when they confirm our own preexisting emotions and ideas.

First, it's important to understand that a dream can come from three sources: self (our own soul), Satan, or God. But how do we differentiate between a genuine confirmation from God, the Enemy's deception, or simply our own heart's desires? The key to understanding the true source of our dreams lies in observing the fruit it produces.

The Fruit Reveals the Seed

A lemon seed won't grow an apple tree. If you were to visit an orchard at a time when new trees are planted, it would be impossible to know what's lying beneath the ground. But as the trees begin to grow and bear fruit, the evidence of the fruit reveals the nature of the seed.

> A dream can come from three sources: self (our own soul), Satan, or God.

This understanding is vital in discerning the source of your dreams. To further develop the fruit tree analogy: You can't recognize an apple tree if you don't first know what an apple is.

To identify the source of your dreams, it is crucial to first understand the nature of God, Satan, and yourself. First John 4:1 warns against false prophets who claim to speak on behalf of God but are, in reality, following Satan. Just as gold can be tested by examining it with vinegar, genuine Christianity can be authenticated by testing it against the nature of God. Real gold is unaffected by vinegar, while fake gold changes color. Similarly, genuine Christianity embodies the ways of God, while false Christianity does not.

As we determine the source of our dreams, let's start by evaluating the fruit produced—the emotions the dreams trigger and the instructions we receive.

The Nature of God

Before I got married, I had a strong desire to find a life partner. I had enjoyed my season of singleness, but felt like I was ready to share my life with someone. Whenever someone I recognized as an eligible bachelor expressed interest in going on a date with me and I had a physical attraction to him, my first question to God was often, "Is this my husband?" Even before I had gotten to know the person, I would begin to imagine what life would be like with him and have dreams that felt so convincing about the potential that he was my soulmate. In the beginning stages, it felt like I was on track to getting married, but in retrospect, those dreams did not come from God. Rather, they were a visual representation of the idol of marriage that had taken root in my heart. I had idolized the idea of companionship, and it had become the focus of my thoughts and meditations, ultimately influencing my dreams.

As I got to know some of these men, it became apparent that

we were completely incompatible. And then I had a realization: My mindset about marriage was unhealthy. I was pursuing it out of pressure, and God would not speak into something that had become an idol in my life. Idols are problematic because they can often become the reflection of our worth and identity, and when they are taken away, life can lose its meaning. Only God is worthy of such weight in our lives. Anything outside of that is likely to sabotage our lives and destiny. For instance, if marriage is an idol, even the smallest argument with your spouse can leave you feeling overtaken by fear and inadequacy, instead of being solution driven.

God did not give me a dream about marriage when I desired it because it would have only validated the idol I had created in my life. It wasn't until I found contentment in being single and trusting in God's timing that He gave me a dream. In this dream, God revealed the qualities of the man He had purposed for me, and the primary trait was selflessness, putting my needs ahead of his own. This reflected the instructions given to husbands in Ephesians 5:25 to love their wives as Christ loved the church and gave Himself for it. As I grew healthier in my desire for marriage, God revealed the character and heart posture of the man He had planned for me. When I woke from the dream, I felt grateful and inspired to become the wife that aligned with God's Word. It was a reminder that marriage is not a sign of my worth, but rather a part of God's will for my life.

All of God's nature is oriented toward building and uplifting His children.[1] We know a dream comes from Him by the positive impact it has on our lives. God's messages aren't meant for superficial purposes such as gossip or for mere information, but always serve His greater purpose.

Discerning Dreams from God

To know God's nature is to have insight about His ways, and the more knowledgeable we are, the easier it becomes to discern whether a dream is from Him. For instance, we may desire something—a new job, a spouse, physical healing, or relational reconciliation—and start having dreams related to that desire, making it challenging to differentiate whether the source is God or ourselves. But as we grow in our knowledge of God, we begin to understand His desires. Desires from God don't come as an obsession or a distraction from our relationship with Him. Instead, they come as a responsibility and burden on our hearts that we are compelled to engage with.

To grow in our knowledge of God, it's essential to begin by studying His Word with the intent of learning about His ways. If we don't have a foundational knowledge of God through the Bible, it becomes challenging to distinguish between the voice of God and that of the Enemy or even ourselves. While the authenticity of the Bible has been debated by many, I believe that if we accept that God is omnipotent, then we must also trust that He would oversee the process of compiling a book that serves as a representation of His voice throughout the centuries. As an omnipresent being, God exists in the past, present, and future simultaneously. He has the power to reveal the realities of each of these realms to us.

I have personally experienced supernatural encounters in my dreams where scriptures I hadn't read before were revealed to me. Through these experiences, I have come to understand that the Bible is truth.

When we approach the study of God's Word with humility

and a genuine desire to grasp His ways, we open ourselves up to supernatural comprehension that can only be attributed to the Holy Spirit's leading.

God is one, meaning that He is indivisible within Himself.[2] His ways are consistent with His written Word, which serves as our defense against deception and manipulation. When Jesus was tempted by Satan, He responded with the written Word of God.[3] Satan then attempted to utilize Scripture taken out of context to tempt Jesus.[4] But Jesus was aware of the Word's meaning and responded with the truth.[5] In the end, Satan was powerless against Jesus.

That conversation between Jesus and Satan teaches us that Jesus had a deep understanding of God's Word. His understanding was not due solely to His identity as God in human form, but it also came through intentional study. We must follow Jesus's example and study the Word of God to identify the dreams from God and resist deception.

As followers of Christ, we should make reading the Word of God a personal practice in our lives. If you are new to studying the Bible, it is wise to seek out a study Bible with commentary to provide context and insight. When studying, there are six key questions we can ask ourselves to deepen our understanding of the text.

- **Who is speaking, or who is the author?**

- **Who is the intended audience?**

- **What is the cultural context?**

- **What is the full context around the events I'm reading about?**

- **What does the text teach me about God?**

- **What personal lesson can I take from this text?**

Regularly reading and studying the Bible will grow our knowledge and understanding of God's Word, enabling us to stand firm in our faith and resist the schemes of the Enemy.

For instance, consider the story of God asking Abraham to sacrifice his son Isaac.[6] At first glance, it may seem shocking and confusing, but with careful study, we can recognize that God wasn't speaking to just anyone—He was speaking to His close friend Abraham, who had a deep relationship with God and trusted His character. Abraham believed that even if he sacrificed his son, God would resurrect him.[7] Understanding the context of the story and the relationship between God and Abraham gives us a different perspective on this text.

By studying and knowing God's nature through His Word, we can also become more discerning of the source of our dreams. Satan will be less able to manipulate or deceive us as we grow in our understanding of God's nature and character.

Here are some practical guidelines to help you distinguish God dreams from others:

- *Consistency with Biblical Values:* Dreams from God will align with the teachings of the Bible, upholding principles of righteousness and integrity. They won't promote actions contrary to God's Word.

- *Avoidance of Sin:* God dreams will never encourage or endorse sinful behavior.

- *Fruit of the Spirit:* God dreams will not affirm negative emotions like envy and fear. They won't support feelings or actions that go against the fruit of the Spirit (love, joy, peace, etc.[8]).

The Nature of Satan

During a flight from Charlotte to Los Angeles, I came across a limited TV series inspired by true events about a serial killer who managed to escape detection due to his benign persona in a small town. Although I felt a spiritual conviction that I shouldn't be watching this, I was hooked on the plot and ignored the prompting of the Holy Spirit. But upon watching it with my husband, we both sensed an inexplicable evil undertone. Later that night, we both had disturbing nightmares and realized that watching the series had opened us up to demonic influences. We both agreed not to watch the show again and prayed for purification and protection over our dreams.

The nightmare I had not only left me feeling anxious and fearful but also depicted one of my dear friends as an evil presence. When I woke up, I realized this dream was not a God dream and it must have been a tool of the Enemy to cause me distress. Perhaps you wonder if this dream was God's way of warning me about my friend. But here's the difference between this type of dream and a warning dream from God: Warning dreams typically bring a sense of calm and direction rather than anxiety and fear. They give us an understanding that God is with us, guiding us and taking care of us, empowering us to move forward with confidence.

In contrast, demonic dreams reflect the nature of Satan, causing fear, torment, anxiety, depression, or loneliness—all of which leave a negative impact on our mental and emotional states. These dreams offer no clarity, direction, or insight, but instead paralyze us with fear and negative thoughts. Most would rather deprive themselves of sleep than go through such an experience. This was the exact thread of emotions I felt after waking up from my dream—consumed by fear and anxiety, with disorganized thoughts about whom I could trust. It was clear to me that the source of this dream was satanic, and I had given him access through the media I consumed. As soon as I rejected the ideas and feelings from the nightmare, they vanished.

The nature of Satan is fundamentally anti-God. His ultimate agenda is to rebel against God and oppose His ways, which led to his fall.[9] Everything he stands for is contrary to God's ways. For instance, the Holy Spirit is referred to as the "Spirit of truth,"[10] whereas Satan is known as the "father of lies."[11] Through our ignorance or neglect, the Enemy may plant demonic dreams that can derail us from our God-given destiny and purpose. In Matthew 13:25, Jesus teaches us how Satan works, by relating a parable of a farmer: "But while men slept, his enemy came and sowed tares among the wheat and went his way." A tare is a weed that resembles wheat in its early stages. If a farmer tries to remove the tares, he might end up killing his own crops. It's only at maturity that he can tell the difference between wheat and tares.

We can learn about dreams from this parable. First, "while men slept" hints that when we are not on guard of our soul's intake, the Enemy finds an opportunity to engage our dreams. Second, he plants in a way that mimics God's work, and the only way we can differentiate is through spiritual maturity—

growing in the knowledge of God's Word, character, and holiness.

If you have been struggling with fear, anxiety, and stress due to a demonic dream, you can release its hold on you by tapping into your God-given authority to step out of agreement with the dream's lie.

Often, this lie comes from the spirit of fear. In 2 Timothy 1:7, Paul wrote, "For God has not given us a spirit of fear, but of power and of love and of a sound mind." We learned earlier that fear as an emotion draws its power from uncertainty, but the *spirit* of fear draws its power from agreement with evil thoughts and imaginations planted by the Enemy. When you agree with these thoughts, they consume you and have power over your actions and decision-making. They can also affect your understanding of God's love, your sense of community, and your ability to reason with wisdom. You may find yourself getting easily offended, entering into a rhythm of self-sabotage, and feeling like the victim in every scenario. This is a gradual process of destruction once the seed of lies has been sown by the Enemy and you agree with it. But you can break free from this cycle by rejecting its narrative and coming into agreement with God's truth.

> The *spirit* of fear draws its power from agreement with evil thoughts and imaginations planted by the Enemy.

God's Word reminds us that fear is not just an emotional response but can manifest as a spirit with an agenda against us. When we operate without power, love, and a sound mind, it's a sign that the spirit of fear has taken root in our lives. Satan's strategy through demonic dreams is to corrupt the messages received through the same channel that God speaks. Understanding God's nature helps us discern areas of deception in our lives and reject lies forged by Satan.

God's intention is not for His Word to diminish the quality of our lives, but for us to experience abundant life. As Jesus said in John 10:10, "The thief comes only to steal and kill and destroy; I have come that they may have life, and have it to the full" (NIV). God desires a satisfying and fulfilling life for us.

Resisting Satan

We've previously touched on Jesus's encounter with Satan in the desert. Now, let's unpack the manipulation behind Satan's temptations. Consider the profound significance of the first recorded temptation faced by Jesus, which was immediately following His forty-day fast, during which He ate nothing.[12] In this pivotal moment, Satan cunningly suggested to Jesus, "If You are the Son of God, command this stone to become bread."[13] At first glance, this temptation may seem harmless; after all, Satan did not offer Him bread that could've been secretly poisoned. Instead, he subtly enticed Jesus to meet His own immediate physical need. But there is a deeper agenda at play here.

The true essence of the Enemy's temptation lay in his desire to undermine Jesus's complete reliance on God's provision and care. By compelling Jesus to take matters into His own hands and miraculously transform the stones into bread, Satan sought to diminish Jesus's trust in the Father's ability to provide for His every need. If Jesus had conceded to this temptation, His future declarations of utter dependence on God would have been compromised. Those sacred words spoken by Jesus, "Very truly I tell you, the Son can do nothing by himself; he can do only what he sees his Father doing,"[14] would have lost their resonance and authenticity. These words encapsulate the profound extent of Jesus's trust, reliance, and dependence on God to guide each step of His earthly journey, rather than being swayed by mere hunger or personal cravings.

This example serves as a poignant testament to the manipulative nature of temptation. It subtly tugs at our deepest desires, weaving intricate webs of deceit in an attempt to divert us from the path of righteousness. It beckons us to prioritize momentary gratification over unwavering trust in God's divine plan for our lives. By highlighting this pivotal moment in Jesus's life, I want to remind us that the power of temptation lies in its ability to tap into our innate desires and exploit them for self-serving purposes.

In essence, temptation is not a random force that unexpectedly descends upon us; it is a calculated infiltration that seeks to exploit our vulnerabilities. It subtly whispers enticing promises and suggestions, luring us away from God's perfect will. Recognizing this truth, we must remain diligent in aligning our desires with the truth of God's Word, resisting the lies and manipulations of the Enemy.

Desires, when not aligned with God's Word and nature, can be misleading and make us vulnerable to the Enemy's influence. This vulnerability can even extend to our dreams, where unchecked desires can allow Satan to plant false images and messages. However, by filtering our thoughts and focusing on Scripture and

God's character, we can resist these deceptive dreams and protect ourselves from the Enemy's tactics.

Resisting Satan requires taking a defensive position, much like a football team's defense aims to stop the opposing offense from scoring. We must not be ignorant of Satan's constant pursuit of opportunities to gain the upper hand in our lives. As we saw with Jesus, after Satan's initial unsuccessful efforts to tempt Him, he did not give up. He patiently waited for another opportune moment.[15] But Satan could never conquer Jesus because Jesus never agreed with his deceitful narrative. When we do not consent to Satan's lies, he cannot score a point.

For instance, if the Enemy is seeking an opportunity to make you fearful, he will wait for a moment when you're vulnerable, perhaps after you've read about a young person's car accident and started contemplating if the same could happen to you. Even though you don't want to, you desire confirmation of your thoughts, and the Enemy is ready to present you with dreams of fatal car accidents, instilling fear in you. However, through prayer and discernment, when you recognize that this dream carries the nature of Satan, you can declare God's Word and promises over your life, such as "I shall not die, but live, and declare the works of the Lord."[16] This is how you resist Satan.

In the realm of spiritual warfare, it is essential to recognize that our thoughts play a significant role. They have a spiritual nature and can profoundly impact our lives. As the apostle Paul encouraged the Corinthians, we are instructed to "take captive every thought to make it obedient to Christ."[17] This underscores the importance of being vigilant and discerning in our thought lives.

When the Enemy gains access to our thoughts, he gains influence over the way we live. The adversary's tactics often involve planting deceptive and destructive ideas in our minds and through our dreams, aiming to lead us astray from God's truth and His plans for our lives. If we succumb to these negative thoughts, they can manifest in our actions, emotions, and overall outlook on life. Resisting Satan is not only a means to protect our dream channels, but it encompasses safeguarding every aspect of our lives.

The Nature of Self

For the flesh lusts against the Spirit, and the Spirit
against the flesh; and these are contrary to one another. . . .
Now the works of the flesh are evident, which are:
adultery, fornication, uncleanness, lewdness, idolatry,
sorcery, hatred, contentions, jealousies, outbursts
of wrath, selfish ambitions, dissensions, heresies, envy,
murders, drunkenness, revelries, and the like.[18]

The natural inclination of the soul is toward the ways of the flesh. This innate tendency is why children can instinctively be deceitful without being taught. Satan loves it when we allow our flesh to dominate our lives, because it makes it easier for him to lead us away from our intended destiny. The apostle Paul recognized this struggle and lived by the principle of dying to self daily.[19] He understood that living according to the ways of the Spirit requires dying to the nature of the flesh daily. Humility is the key to acknowledging our weaknesses and surrendering them to Christ so we are not manipulated by them. It is important to honestly identify areas of weakness and not give them a platform in our lives, labeling them as the voice of God.

As a pastor, I have encountered numerous instances where people have used the name of God to justify selfish ambitions, envy, lustful motives, and similar vices instead of surrendering them to God. I have heard stories of people who started businesses out of envy of others, allowing themselves to be distracted by social media and creating strategies to compete with those who posed no threat. Unfortunately, this lack of transparency and self-awareness also plays out in our dreams. When the lust of the flesh consumes a person's thinking, their dreams may reflect these thoughts and desires while they sleep. It becomes dangerous when we assume that every dream is from God without examining its nature and fruit. We must ask ourselves, *Does the message of this dream glorify God, or does it glorify the lusts of my flesh?* By evaluating the source of the dream's message and what it glorifies, we can avoid being led astray from God's will.

God cautions us about being led by dreams that are evidence of the lusts of our flesh. He identifies such dreams as "dreams which you cause to be dreamed"[20] because their source is not from God but from within ourselves.

Now, not every dream from our own desires is evil. Sometimes dreams come from what we're thinking about, and not all thoughts are wrong. For example, one night we found a plumbing issue at home, and my husband was thinking about how to fix it. That night, he dreamed about the plumbing issue affecting our entire home. It wasn't a dream from God, but it wasn't a bad dream either; it was just a dream from his own thoughts. This shows why we must be mindful about what we think before going to sleep. Instead of going to bed troubled by problems, we can invite God to help us find solutions. When we surrender our thoughts like this, they become a kind of prayer—one that God might answer through our dreams.

Embrace the Journey

As you become better at discerning the sources of your dreams, I want to encourage you by reminding you that this is a journey. The truth is, you do not need to become an expert in discerning the source of your dreams overnight. There is no finish line of mastery. It is a continuous journey that requires surrender and humility before God, who will partner with you to provide insight. God's desire is for you to know His voice and be able to discern your dreams accurately, distinguishing those that come from Him. Embrace this journey of growing in recognizing His voice, and rest in the fact that He is with you even now.

> *Heavenly Father, I come to You today asking for Your guidance and direction as I seek to understand the source of my dreams. I know that You have a purpose and a plan for my life, and I trust that You desire for me to recognize and discern the messages You communicate to me through my dreams. Help me to understand the hidden meaning behind these symbols and to be open to the wisdom and direction that You offer. Thank You for Your continued love and guidance in my life. I pray this in Jesus's name, amen.*

Reflection Questions

1. What suggestions for studying the Bible stood out to you, and why did they resonate with you?

2. Consider the dreams you've had recently. Can you identify the sources based on what we've discussed in this chapter? For any dreams that you're still unsure about, pray about them today and ask God for wisdom.

FIVE

TYPES OF DREAMS

And Daniel could understand visions
and dreams of all kinds.

—Daniel 1:17, NIV

The realm of dreams is rich and diverse, offering insights into different aspects of our lives—including experiences that many people have in common. Maybe you've talked to others and realized you've had dreams eerily similar to theirs. In this chapter, we'll explore six common types of dreams: directional dreams, impartation dreams, strategy dreams, encouragement dreams, warning dreams, and watchman dreams. While it's not an exhaustive list, it provides a solid foundation for understanding the ways God communicates with us through our dreams. Dreams can contain multiple unique details, but there is always a profound theme that conveys the message.

For example, during my pregnancy, I was anxious about the challenges of becoming a first-time mother, specifically in the area of breastfeeding. Questions would plague my mind like, *Will my baby have difficulty breastfeeding? Will I know how to*

breastfeed? Will she feel relaxed around me? But in God's goodness, I had a dream where I was feeding my newborn daughter
with ease, feeling a deep sense of calm and a beautiful bond with
her. This dream brought me comfort and reassurance, and while
its principal theme was encouragement, I could have understood
it as an instructional dream telling me that I didn't need to be
overly concerned about hiring a lactation consultant. Understanding the theme of a dream can guide us in comprehending
what God desires to say to us through it.

As we further explore the different types of dreams, it's worth
noting that while we'll examine different examples of dreams
under each category, the symbols and visuals in your dreams
are often unique to you, the dreamer.
Dream interpretation is not a one-
size-fits-all process. While there are
some symbols that have universal significance, such as water representing
the Holy Spirit and fire representing
purification or judgment, many sym-
bols are personal and unique to the individual. For example, seeing a specific animal may hold a special meaning to one person
based on their experiences and cultural background. When trying to interpret or understand a dream, it's important to consider
the dreamer's personal circumstances and experiences during
their waking life. Only then can the dream be fully understood
and applied to them because no two dreamers have identical experiences, and as such, the discernment of symbols and themes in
a dream can be a unique and personal process.

> Dream
> interpretation
> is not a
> one-size-fits-
> all process.

In addition, as we grow in our faith and relationship with
God, our understanding of dream symbolism may evolve, allow-

ing for deeper and more meaningful interpretations. In Matthew chapter 13, Jesus spoke in parables to a multitude of people, but the true meaning of the parable was hidden from them. Then His disciples came to Him and asked, "Why do You speak to them in parables?"[1] Jesus responded, saying, "Because it has been given to you to know the mysteries of the kingdom of heaven, but to them it has not been given"[2] However, Jesus had a deeper connection with His disciples, and He revealed the meaning of the parable to them.[3]

As it relates to dreams, this shows that the more intimacy we build with God, the clearer our understanding of the message in our dreams becomes. Dreams can be considered parables of the night, and like Jesus's parables, they hold crucial divine truths that God wants us to discern. Through cultivating a deeper relationship with God, we can more fully comprehend the rich symbolism and imagery presented in our dreams, and receive them as blessings. While some people may struggle to understand the meaning of their dreams, those who have deep intimacy with God can receive more profound revelations, conveyed in a memorable, concise, and impactful manner.

Directional Dreams

Your word is a lamp to guide my feet
and a light for my path.[4]

Directional dreams are God's way of communicating with us and providing us with clarity and direction. These dreams often reveal our unique calling and purpose and guide us toward the path we are meant to take in the different seasons of our lives.

When we have a directional dream, we may see ourselves doing things we never imagined were possible, or find ourselves being directed toward a different place in our lives. But it is essential to remember that without God's Word, we may inadvertently stray from the path that leads us toward our ultimate purpose. His Word provides us with the guidance we need to remain aligned with our destiny. It serves as a beacon of light to help us navigate the challenges and uncertainties we may face in life. By staying true to our faith and remaining open to His communications, we can trust that we are on the right path and that our lives have a greater purpose. Living a life directed by God is fulfilling and enriching. When we discover and walk in alignment with our true calling, we live a life of significance and impact.

Before I embarked on my journey as a pastor, I never saw myself in this role. Although I yearned to serve God through a life of purpose and influence, I had envisioned serving Him in other ways. As a child, I aspired to become a lawyer and a talk-show host. As I grew older, my dreams began to evolve. It was not until I started experiencing vivid dreams of speaking to vast crowds that I realized there might be more to my purpose and calling. These dreams ignited a spark within me, awakening a desire to discover what God knows about me that I may be unaware of. I yearned to seek His guidance and direction.

As I began this journey of self-discovery, I had even more profound dreams that revealed God's calling upon my life. These dreams brought me clarity and direction, making it evident that God had a specific purpose for me. I realized that although my initial interests and passions were essential, this newfound discovery would enable me to fulfill the calling of God upon my life, and it has transformed my life in ways that I never thought possible.

One of the most impactful directional dreams I've ever had was a vivid vision of a place in heaven. Surrounded by several people, I suddenly heard a voice booming, "Whom shall I send? And who will go for us?" Without hesitation, I fervently waved my hand high, pleading with each repetition, "Send me! Send me!" At this point, I was directly singled out by the voice, and God revealed my divine assignment. He instructed me to descend through the waters wherein lay a section that needed to be broken open. Once found, I was to open it and be transported directly to hell, where my role as an ambassador of God would begin. There I found numerous candles on a shelf that weren't lit, but when I touched each candle, it immediately ignited. As each one flamed, the person the candle belonged to was freed from the grips of darkness and led to the kingdom of God.

During this process, God reassured me not to be afraid, even if Satan caught wind of the work I was engaging in in his kingdom. Before the Enemy could even touch me, I would be taken back home by God Himself. I followed every instruction to the letter, and all that I envisioned unfolded before my eyes. As I worked in hell to free the individuals trapped by the Enemy's chains, Satan eventually discovered what was transpiring, and naturally, he came for me, and his minions formed an army against me. But then something wild happened: I was suddenly transported back into our world on earth, where I interacted with strangers speaking different languages, yet we understood each other. From there, Satan and his army caught sight of me, but before they could take me, God brought me back home to heaven where I woke up from the dream.

Although complex in nature, the dream's meaning became clear with the Holy Spirit's guidance and proper interpretation techniques (which we'll explore further in chapter 6). The questions asked—"Whom shall I send? And who will go for us?"— echoed the exact inquiry the prophet Isaiah responded to in the Bible when receiving his commission from God,[5] setting the dream's tone for bringing direction. Additionally, the water and its subsequent breaking represented my own birth, similar to how a mother's water breaks before delivery. The dream revealed insight into comprehending the primary reasoning behind my birth. In chapter 1, we established the significance of God's knowledge of us before our birth. Through this dream, God revealed what He had always known about me, even before my entrance into the world.

Being in hell and the experience of igniting people's candles by a simple touch represented my mission to lead individuals from darkness to light. The theme of darkness generally refers to ignorance, oppression, and Satan's kingdom; when I illuminated their path, however, their journey toward God's kingdom and truth could begin. Scripture refers to children of God as "children of light,"[6] and the dream reinforced my assignment to serve as a beacon of light to guide others to discovering their path and calling in Christ Jesus.

As the Lord revealed to me, my calling involves conveying His word and leading individuals toward truth and a relationship with Him. This book is a testament to that calling and serves to enlighten people on the significance of dreams in fostering a deeper intimacy with God and living fulfilled lives. I believe that the dream's depiction of me being in hell did not denote my literal presence in that location. Rather, it indicated that God's purpose for my life requires me to navigate through dark places to impart His light by teaching His Word.

The adversary's pursuit of me in the dream represented spiritual warfare manifested through the Enemy's attempt to launch attacks against me. But as evidenced in Isaiah 54:17, no weapon formed against me shall prosper. Despite my physical encounters with Satan in waking life, his schemes remained powerless against me. The dream also illustrated a moment where, despite individuals speaking different languages, we were able to comprehend one another, signifying my impact and influence across diverse cultures. This is now palpable through the wide array of translations of the sermons and teachings I deliver.

Lastly, God's act of bringing me back to heaven before the Enemy could reach me affirmed His unwavering protection and provision over my life. Regardless of the circumstances I may encounter, God's shield against the Enemy and His divinely ordained plan for me will never falter. When my assignment concludes, He will call me home.

This directional dream was incredibly powerful and moved me to my core. It remains a constant reminder that when we seek God's guidance, He will send us in the right direction to serve Him and fulfill our true purpose in this life. It is a testament that we should never be afraid when following His commands, and that even when walking through the valley of the shadow of death, He will always be with us and protect us from our enemies.

The dream's instruction was multifaceted, providing me both a specific and broader understanding of my purpose as a minister. God illuminated the central focus of my ministry, while simultaneously revealing the extent of His covering in my life.

This dream was transformational and set in motion a chain of events. It is crucial to note that everyone's directional dreams in terms of their calling are unique, and may vary in their level of drama or intensity. Some dreamers may see themselves performing the very thing God has called them to do, while others may receive the same understanding in a parabolic sense. Regardless, the overarching objective of such dreams is to provide us with a profound sense of direction and purpose in life.

Directional dreams have the potential to reveal our geographical paths as well. Our lives are never random, even as far back as our birthplace. Similarly, certain stages of life may require a move to an unfamiliar location to fulfill the divine purpose assigned to us based on our identity in God and the calling on our lives.

For me, pursuing a career in law was once my aspiration, and I had planned to study in London after completing high school. Since I was the youngest child and only daughter, the idea of being close to home was desirable for both my mother and me. But God instructed me to go to California, and despite our initial plans, my mother and I prayerfully considered this new direction. Since then, the evidence of this divinely guided decision has been extraordinary, manifesting through the fruit of my life.

The Bible consistently shows God's pattern of directing His people toward a specific location for a particular purpose. For instance, God promised blessings to Abraham, contingent upon his relocation to a specific region that God would reveal to him.[7] When the apostle Paul and his companions aimed to preach the gospel in Asia, the Holy Spirit disallowed their plans. They made another attempt to preach in Bithynia, but once again, the Holy Spirit did not permit it. It is important to understand that our perception of what is good may not always align with God's will and purpose for our lives. As such, the Holy Spirit did not allow them to settle for their standard of good but rather directed them to God's standard—alignment with His will and plan concerning their lives. After this redirection, He gave them a vision that carried a clear instruction on where they should travel and preach the gospel, in Macedonia.[8]

Similarly, dreams can serve as a conduit through which God communicates directional instructions to us, as evidenced when Jacob received guidance to return home.[9] It is pertinent to note that these instructions may come with utmost clarity, or we may visualize ourselves in a particular city or country but not know where that place is. By committing these dreams to prayer, God often confirms His message in due course.

Impartation Dreams

That night the LORD appeared to Solomon
in a dream, and God said, "What do you want?
Ask, and I will give it to you!"[10]

Impartation dreams are extraordinary encounters with God or an angel to impart supernatural realities to the dreamer. They often come with an endowment of the gifts of the Holy Spirit, such as wisdom, knowledge, faith, healings, miracles, etc.,[11] to equip the dreamer with what's necessary to fulfill their purpose in God.

The message received in an impartation dream naturally unfolds in our waking lives without any action required for its manifestation. Whether the dream involves a visit from an angel or the Lord Jesus, it serves as a powerful catalyst for growth and change in one's life.

One of the most famous dreams in the Bible is King Solomon's impartation dream. One night, shortly after becoming king, he had an encounter with God, who offered to give him anything he desired. Solomon requested wisdom to equip him as an effective leader, and God granted his request, along with great wealth, possessions, and honor. As a result of this dream, Solomon became renowned for his wisdom and was widely recognized as one of the greatest sages in history. Some of his teachings and insights were recorded in the book of Proverbs, which remains a cornerstone of Wisdom Literature.

In my experience and through the study of the Word, I've learned that impartation dreams don't happen at random. They are the result of a heart that earnestly seeks God above all else.[12] A heart that is willing to sacrifice worldly pleasures to pursue the will of God. King Solomon's encounter with God through his impartation dream serves as a powerful example of a selfless and humble heart that attracts the empowerment of God.[13] At the time of his encounter, Solomon embodied these selfless traits, which were evident in his request to the Lord. Despite having been given the opportunity to ask for personal gain, he was purpose driven and asked for wisdom to become an effective leader for his people.

It's important to remember that the absence of impartation dreams is not an indication that God is not pleased with us or that we are not seeking Him with purity of heart. God can impart wisdom to us in unique and individualized ways that are aligned with His purpose for our lives. And God equips us with the unique resources and abilities we need to fulfill His purpose in various ways. We must trust both the wisdom of God and the integrity of His nature, and approach our journey with faith. Our walk with God is not always easy, and we may face setbacks or challenges, but we must trust that God is working everything out for our good[14] and that His plan for our lives is perfect.

Impartation can take many forms. While Solomon received an impartation of wisdom through a dream from God, Joshua received his impartation when Moses, his spiritual leader, laid hands on him.[15] This act was sanctioned by God and allowed the same possibilities that Moses walked in with God to become evident in the life of Joshua.

I have experienced several impartation dreams throughout my life. One impartation dream was an encounter with the Lord Jesus that healed my physical body. Prior to the dream, I had been experiencing pain in my left breast, and when I examined it, I felt a lump. I sought the Lord for healing, and in a dream, He came to me and pulled from the affected area what looked like a worm. I woke up with both the pain and the lump gone; the threat to my health was healed through this encounter. This experience reinforced my faith in God's ability to use impartation dreams to meet specific needs and equip us for His purpose.

Strategy Dreams

In all your ways acknowledge him,
and he will make straight your paths.[16]

Strategy dreams are powerful interventions from God that offer divine solutions to existing or potential personal or professional challenges. They differ from impartation dreams because they do require us to take the insights or revelations from the dream and actively apply the wisdom to the specific areas of our lives that it addresses. These dreams provide a pathway to advancement, promotion, or prosperity in our lives. God desires that we live in abundance, and understanding that He is the source of everything we have helps us to embrace Him as our provider. Even King David, despite his great wealth and influence as a king, recognized and acknowledged God as the source of it all, declaring, "The LORD is my shepherd; I shall not want."[17] It's important to note that God blesses us without bringing sorrow.[18] So His blessings are often the evidence of a person who will not be controlled by them, who will not forsake integrity to maintain in his or her own strength what was made possible by God.

It's essential to acknowledge that God provides divine wisdom through strategy dreams that bring solutions we need in order to overcome challenges and advance in our lives. The invention of the sewing machine is a fascinating example of how a strategy dream led to significant advancements in both the apparel industry and personal life. As I mentioned earlier, inventor Elias Howe had a dream that became the catalyst for the development of the sewing machine.[19] This visionary dream ultimately led him out of poverty and into a life of affluence.

Similarly, Madam C. J. Walker's story is an inspiring example of how strategy dreams can lead to life-changing transformations. Suffering from hair loss due to a scalp condition, she was moved by her plight to seek divine intervention. A strategy dream provided her with a feasible solution, revealing to her a combination of ingredients that could remedy her scalp condition and stimulate hair growth. She created a successful line of hair care products that eventually helped countless women regain their hair's health and beauty.[20]

These stories underscore the importance of recognizing the significance of these dreams and how they can help us tap into the divine power of God. When we seek His guidance through our dreams, we unlock the wealth of wisdom and strategic insights that can ultimately lead to our personal growth and the betterment of society.

I have had the privilege of experiencing the guidance of strategy dreams firsthand. A couple of years ago, I closed a business deal that earned me a sum of money, and rather than let it sit in my account, I wanted to invest it wisely. As I started studying and researching the stock market, I realized that I lacked confidence in making investment decisions. I turned to prayer, asking God for His guidance on how to make the best use of my funds. I started having a series of strategy dreams that provided me with insight on which stocks to buy and the right time to sell them. These strategy dreams were remarkably precise, and within a few months, my initial investment had yielded over 300 percent. Not only did this bring financial increases to me personally, but it also benefited my family and friends with whom I shared these strategies.

As biblical scholars will attest to, one of the most compelling accounts of the power of strategy dreams in the Bible is found in the story of Joseph.[21] He was a prisoner who, through the interpretation of a strategy dream, was promoted to become second-in-command over all of Egypt.

In the story, it was Pharaoh, the king of Egypt, who received the dream. Despite not worshipping God, he was able to recognize the dream's significance as it reoccurred with a similar message. But he was unable to interpret it. When he sought someone to interpret his dream, Joseph was brought before him and given wisdom by God to interpret it. The interpretation revealed what would soon happen, and Joseph suggested what the people ought to do in order to preserve food in the land in preparation for a future famine.

The story of Joseph highlights how God uses strategy dreams to reveal divine plans and purposes that are beyond our natural comprehension. In this case, it led to the salvation of an entire nation from famine. It's a powerful reminder that seeking God's wisdom through strategy dreams can lead to blessings and progress beyond what we could ever imagine.

Strategy dreams serve as a testament to God's willingness to work alongside us in addressing our challenges. They remind us of the significance of seeking God's wisdom and guidance in every facet of our lives, and display the remarkable potency of dreams as a vehicle for receiving divine insight and knowledge.

Encouragement Dreams

I sought the Lord, and He heard me,
and delivered me from all my fears.[22]

To be encouraged is to receive inspiration that empowers us to overcome our fears and take bold action. Throughout life, we are likely to encounter many challenges that cause us to feel fearful. But these challenges often provide an opportunity for us to discover our true potential in God.

Encouragement can come in many different forms, including dreams, which serve as a divine confirmation that we are on the right path. Dreams offer us the imagery and messages we need to overcome our feelings of fear, replacing them instead with hope and determination. Through this encouragement, we can move forward with a newfound sense of confidence and purpose.

Dreams of encouragement, like the one Jacob had in Genesis 28, offer a beacon of hope and reassurance when we find ourselves lost or afraid. These dreams are a reminder of God's promises and plans for our lives, and they provide a fresh perspective on our situation. Jacob had been running from his vengeful twin brother, Esau, but God's promise to him in his dream gave him the courage and faith for the journey ahead.

Jacob's dream was a message from God that he was not alone in his troubles. God promised to guide him back to his homeland and watch over him every step of the way. This dream gave Jacob hope and a renewed sense of purpose and direction. When he woke up, he knew that God was with him and that he would be okay.

Encouragement dreams like Jacob's can inspire us to take action as well. They can motivate us to trust in God's promises and seek His guidance in our lives. Just as Jacob set up a memorial stone to mark the spot where he met God,[23] we can also mark important moments in our lives where God has spoken to us through dreams or other signs. These encouragements are reminders to keep our faith strong, even in difficult times.

Encouraging dreams can manifest themselves in various ways, such as personal messages that are a result of a divine encounter or through imagery and symbolism to convey the same message. Though they may take different forms, their purpose remains consistent—to reassure you that God is with you and to give you hope and courage to move forward with optimistic anticipation.

Warning Dreams

There is a way that seems right to a man,
but its end is the way of death.[24]

Warning dreams serve as a divine guidance mechanism, steering us away from impending danger that we may be headed toward without realizing it. These types of dreams are intended to protect the dreamer or create awareness of involvement in activities that could be potentially harmful, be it physically or spiritually. Warning dreams often include vivid, intense, and reoccurring images in order for us to pay close attention and heed the warning conveyed through these dreams to avoid undesirable outcomes.

It is suggested that President Abraham Lincoln, who served as the sixteenth president of the United States, had a warning dream prior to his death. His friend Ward Hill Lamon recalled the vivid dream Lincoln had of his assassination ten days before it happened. In the dream, he walked through the White House and heard mourners crying in another room. When he asked a soldier standing guard who had died, the soldier replied, "The President. He was killed by an assassin."[25] Tragically, days later, Lincoln was assassinated at Ford's Theatre in Washington, D.C. It was believed that Lincoln saw his dream as a premonition of his death. I can't help but wonder if he saw this as a warning about the Enemy's plans against his life. What if he had acted on this information and acknowledged it as a security risk, canceling plans that were made known to the public and taking some time to be in prayer for further insight into the dream? Would his fate have been different? While we may never know for sure, my personal experience and the experiences of others with warning dreams have shown that it is paramount to carefully consider the details provided through prayer and to take action. By being humble and curious, we become receptive to the guidance imparted through warning dreams.

There are also various examples of warning dreams in the Bible. One such instance is when King Abimelech had intentions to sleep with Sarah, Abraham's wife. Abraham, fearing for his safety, had presented her as his sister to Abimelech, who then summoned her. But in God's mercy, Abimelech was visited in a dream that served as a warning to prevent him from committing adultery with the wife of a man in covenant with God and thereby bringing a curse upon his household.

> But God came to Abimelech in a dream by night, and said to him, "Indeed you are a dead man because of the woman whom you have taken, for she is a man's wife." But Abimelech had not come near her; and he said, "Lord, will You slay a righteous nation also? Did he not say to me, 'She is my sister'? And she, even she herself said, 'He is my brother.' In the integrity of my heart and innocence of my hands I have done this." And God said to him in a dream, "Yes, I know that you did this in the integrity of your heart. For I also withheld you from sinning against Me; therefore I did not let you touch her. Now therefore, restore the man's wife; for he is a prophet, and he will pray for you and you shall live. But if you do not restore her, know that you shall surely die, you and all who are yours.[26]

Abimelech's dream was a direct encounter with God, who cautioned him to return Abraham's wife to him before he suffered destruction. Similarly, warning dreams serve the purpose of providing guidance in areas where we may be ignorant or are making decisions without insight. Such decisions could potentially bring destruction personally, professionally, or in other ways.

In addition to alerting us to physical harm, warning dreams can also caution us about spiritual dangers. Today's culture is witnessing a mixture of Christianity and New Age practices, such as spiritual cleansing with sage, crystal usage, opening the third eye, and tarot card reading. These practices are often demonic gateways that lead to a gestational period of oppression and torment in one's life. Unfortunately, many fail to recognize these dangers and notice where they have opened the door to spiritual harm.

Throughout the years, I've witnessed people afflicted with demonic spirits become delivered and healed. But while they were afflicted, they had a recurring pattern of dreams. These dreams depicted car crashes while driving, representing an impending threat of destruction.

Other dreams involved being molested by seemingly known individuals or strange creatures, even though the dreamer wasn't struggling with sexual addiction or experiencing that trauma in their waking life. These types of dreams can be unraveled by understanding the spiritual significance of sex. Physically, sex leads to a oneness of flesh,[27] which spiritually signifies intimacy. When we commit our lives to God, we become one with Him in spirit.[28] Anything outside of Him represents a form of spiritual adultery, and those who lust after such things are considered adulterous by God.[29] Hence, whether one willingly or unknowingly engages in demonic practices, it creates agreement with the kingdom of darkness, which represents a form of intimacy with Satan. Thus, some dreams that seem graphic may be warning dreams from God revealing the harm one's spirit has been exposed to from indulging in demonic practices. The purpose of these dreams is not to instill fear but rather to guide the dreamer toward spiritual well-being. However, if a graphic dream triggers traumatic events or causes debilitating fear rather than sparking curiosity in the dreamer and a desire for clarity about its meaning, it's likely that the source isn't God.

Another example of such dreams would be being chased by a dog, despite not being afraid of dogs. In the Bible, dogs are often used to represent unclean things,[30] and some believe this kind of dream signifies gluttony. In this sense, it represents spiritual adultery—feeding on anything that appears spiritual without considering its risks and dangers to one's life.

When these types of dreams become recurring, it is a sign that one should pay attention to their warnings. Through prayer and humility, the dreamer can ask the Lord to reveal anything they may have exposed themselves to that has opened a door to a demonic covenant working against their life. The Bible promises us goodness and mercy all the days of our lives.[31] While some dreams may represent God's goodness, warning dreams often represent God's mercy toward us. They serve to make us aware of potential harm in order to bring us out of harm's way. It is essential to heed such warnings to protect ourselves spiritually and physically.

Watchman Dreams

For thus has the Lord said to me:
"Go, set a watchman, let him declare what he sees."[32]

The term *watchman* has its roots in the Hebrew word ṣāpâ, which means to keep watch or to spy out potential dangers.[33] Though the word suggests a certain gender, the focus is the position and function. In biblical times, watchmen were appointed to keep watch over a city or nation, alerting its inhabitants of potential or impending danger. These watchmen existed in both the natural and spiritual realms, as we see with the prophet Ezekiel, whom God appointed as a watchman for the Israelites during his time.[34] When God forewarned of impending danger, Ezekiel warned the people, and those who heeded the warnings received redemption.

Being a spiritual watchman involves having God-given insight to discern the Enemy's plans for the territories allocated to the watchman by God—these territories include family, workplace, relationships, small groups, etc. Unlike warning dreams that convey messages specifically for the dreamer, watchman dreams contain insights regarding those assigned to the dreamer's life. Then through prayer, the watchman can prevent and counteract these evil plans. For instance, there was a moment when Jesus interacted with His disciple Peter, sharing insight into Satan's plans to bring Peter down by tempting him to deny Jesus. Despite Peter's confidence that he would never deny Christ, Jesus knew the extent of the danger and revealed His strategy to secure Peter's faith. He simply said, "But I have prayed for you."[35] Jesus's prayer was an assurance to Peter that even though he would fall for Satan's trap, Satan's ultimate agenda would fail because Jesus had prayed for Peter, supernaturally equipping him with grace to overcome.

A key function of being a watchman is gaining foresight into the Enemy's traps and using the power of prayer to thwart his agenda. God often reveals this knowledge through divine messages, such as watchman dreams, which unveil either God's plan or the Enemy's agenda that necessitates partnership in prayer to either bring forth or block.

Some may question why God does not simply handle these agendas on His own. But the story of Elijah offers insight into the necessity of partnership with God's will. After Elijah declared a drought lasting three and a half years, God instructed him to bring forth another word that the drought would be over.[36] This was God's word, His purpose, and Elijah was His instrument to declare and bring it forth. However, Elijah's role didn't end there, for Scripture recounts that "Elijah was a man with a nature like ours, and he prayed earnestly."[37] Through prayer, Elijah placed himself in a position to partner with the will of God. This reflects God's entrustment in humankind to carry out His activities on earth.[38] God's agenda cannot be fully established without our agreement, for He has given dominion over the earth to humanity, necessitating partnership. Throughout the Scriptures, an ongoing partnership between God and humanity is evident, illustrating this collaboration required to fulfill His agenda. Before Jesus was born, God raised up a prophetess named Anna, who prayed unceasingly for the arrival of the Lord.[39] This emphasizes the urgency of partnering with God's will through prayer.

All of us are called to be watchmen of various territories, beginning with our families. As we grow in our walks with God, He may enlarge our sphere of influence, leading us to have dreams concerning our communities, cities, jobs, nations, and much more. Watchman dreams reveal the breadth of the territory that God has called us to watch over.

I once had a watchman dream concerning my brother. In the dream, I saw a printed calendar with a date circled in red, and it was revealed that the Enemy had a plan against my brother's life. Upon awakening, I wrote down the date and shared it with him, and began praying for his protection. Several weeks later, my brother noticed he was being followed by a car with several men bearing the characteristics of a dangerous gang. He attempted to evade them by making random turns, but they persistently followed. This alerted him to the high possibility of a robbery attempt. He eventually escaped them and made it back home safely.

After he shared his experience with me, I cross-referenced the date with my earlier notes, confirming the insight God had given me. Through prayer, we had partnered with God in stopping the Enemy's plan and protecting my brother's life. This serves as a testament to the potency

> Dreams are not ends in themselves; they should serve as a prompt for action.

of watchman dreams and the power of prayer in partnering with God's will.

Sharing watchman dreams requires discernment. If your dream includes time-sensitive elements like a specific date or incident, it is advisable to share it with the person it's about. This can help them stay vigilant and mindful of the details from the dream. But if the dream lacks insights or doesn't give clear instructions, it's better not to share it. This way, you avoid making the person worried or scared. For example, if your dream suggests a certain person might die, don't be quick to share. Instead, spend time praying for them. Declare God's promises related to long life, believing in the power of God's Word during prayer to thwart the plans of the Enemy.

Just as God uses partners to carry out His divine agenda, the Enemy requires partners to execute his plans. The men who were following my brother were not mere coincidence; they were vulnerable to being used as instruments of Satan's agenda. Through prayer, we can stop the plans of the Enemy and prevent the horrific images from playing out in real life.

It is essential to remember that dreams are not ends in themselves; they should serve as a prompt for action. When we receive a message from a dream, it should motivate us to act.

Heavenly Father, You are the giver of all good gifts, and I thank You for the precious gift of dreams that offer me insights, direction, and guidance. I thank You for the different kinds of dreams that can warn me of danger, reveal hidden truths about my situations, and call me to action. Lord, I confess that sometimes I may not be as sensitive to Your voice as I should be. I ask that You help me become more aware of the dreams You give me, so I can more easily understand them and use them to carry out Your will for my life. I ask for Your guidance and direction as I seek to interpret and understand my dreams. May I approach them with humility and openness to Your leading. I pray this in the name of Jesus, who taught us to pray, saying: "Our Father in heaven, hallowed be Your name. Your kingdom come. Your will be done on earth as it is in heaven. Give us this day our daily bread. And forgive us our debts, as we forgive our debtors. And do not lead us into temptation, but deliver us from the evil one."[40] In Jesus's name, amen.

Reflection Questions

1. Can you recall experiencing any of the dream themes discussed in this chapter? How did they influence your life?

2. What specific kinds of dreams are you currently seeking from God?

SIX

THE INTERPRETATION
OF DREAMS

Do not interpretations belong to God?

—Genesis 40:8

I
n January 2018, I had the opportunity to co-write, co-produce, and co-direct a short film that was featured in the Los Angeles Movie Awards. We were thrilled to win the Audience Award, especially because this was my first experience working on a film. But as I looked back on the journey of making this film, I realized that there were so many unseen faces that played a critical role in bringing the movie to life and conveying its message to the audience. Before this experience, I used to skip over the credits for categories like best sound mixing, best production design, and best costume design when watching award ceremonies, believing them to be irrelevant. But now I know that every element of a film contributes to its overall impact.

From the sound effects to the editing, color grading, costume design, and movie score, every aspect must work in harmony to tell the story effectively. For example, a romance film with a horror movie score or actors dressed in spikes would leave the audience confused, even if the acting and the story were clear. The same is true for our dreams: To fully understand their message, we must consider all their elements.

My family and friends have long called me "Joseph, the dream interpreter" because of my ability to understand and interpret the messages conveyed through dreams. Like the biblical Joseph, I believe that this gift is not merely a natural talent or insight, but a result of being in relationship with God. The true gift is the Holy Spirit, while we are just the instrument He flows through.

As Joseph himself said, "Do not interpretations belong to God?"[1] In other words, it is ultimately God who reveals the meaning of our dreams, and our role is simply to be open and receptive to His guidance.

When I was younger, dream interpretation came easily to me. Whether it was my own dreams or the dreams of others, I could immediately discern their significance. But as I grew older, it became more challenging. I eventually realized that the shift happened so that I would not simply be an instrument for dream interpretation, but would teach others as well. So, in my adult years, the Lord began to teach me not just how to interpret my own dreams, but also how to train others to understand the messages that God reveals to them through their dreams. This required me to learn and apply practical steps and tools for dream interpretation, even as I relied on the Holy Spirit for guidance and truth.

Dream interpretation is an important skill for every believer to develop. By learning how to understand the messages God sends us through our dreams, we can deepen our relationship with Him, gain wisdom and insight into our lives, and help others to do the same.

As I've delved into the Word of God, I've come to see that multiplication is a key theme throughout Scripture. It's woven into the very fabric of God's nature and character. For example, when God created humanity, His first instruction to them was to "be fruitful and multiply."[2] This command was not just about physical offspring, but about multiplying everything that God had entrusted to them. And when Jesus came to earth, He didn't just focus on building a following of individual disciples. He selected a team of apostles who would continue His mission after He left, and He promised that they would do even greater things than He had done.[3] This speaks to God's desire for multiplication, for the spread of the gospel and the works of the Holy Spirit through many hands and many hearts.

The same is true for dream interpretation. As I teach others how to understand and engage the Holy Spirit in their own dreams, I am multiplying the understanding that God has given me. I am sharing what I have received so that others can benefit from it, and in turn, they can teach others. It's a beautiful cycle of grace, generosity, and multiplication that reflects the heart of God and His desire to bless and empower His children.

> Every element in a dream has meaning.

As mentioned earlier, every element in a dream has meaning. This is especially evident in the story of Joseph, who was gifted with insight and understanding in this area by God. As we study Joseph's approach to dream interpretation, we can see that he didn't simply give an isolated message that lacked cohesiveness with the dream itself. Rather, he was able to grasp the symbolism and significance of each element in the dream, and weave them together into a coherent message. We might disregard a dream as insignificant or nonsensical, when a message from God is actually hidden in the symbols.

Let's examine how Joseph addressed dream interpretation.

While in prison, Joseph was approached by a former cup-bearer to Pharaoh, who had been imprisoned alongside him. The cupbearer recounted a dream to Joseph, and Joseph was able to provide a comprehensive interpretation that tied each element of the dream together. This attention to detail and sensitivity to symbolism is what sets effective dream interpretation apart from surface-level analysis. By diving deep into the imagery and language of a dream, we can unlock profound truths and insights that can change the course of our lives.

> So the chief cup-bearer told Joseph his dream first. "In my dream," he said, "I saw a grapevine in front of me. The vine had three branches that began to bud and blossom, and soon it produced clusters of ripe grapes. I was holding Pharaoh's wine cup in my hand, so I took a cluster of grapes and squeezed the juice into the cup. Then I placed the cup in Pharaoh's hand."
>
> "This is what the dream means," Joseph said. "The three branches represent three days. Within three days Pharaoh will lift you up and restore you to your position as his chief cup-bearer."[4]

It's fascinating to see how the interpretation of a dream can hinge on the symbolism and imagery contained within it. In the case of Joseph's interpretation of the cupbearer's dream, we can see how each element of the dream worked together in harmony to convey a specific message.

For example, when Joseph heard about the three branches in the dream, he recognized that they represented three days. This was connected to the symbol of "ripe grapes," which was significant because the cupbearer's primary responsibility was handling the king's cup. Wine, which is typically made from grapes, is a common beverage served in such a cup. As such, the image of three branches producing the wine that went in the cup that was in the cupbearer's hand became a powerful metaphor to communicate the message that the cupbearer would be reinstated to his former position in three days.

This example highlights the importance of paying attention to what's in your dream—the symbols and details—in order to understand its message. Then you can gain a deeper understanding of the messages God may be speaking to you.

Dream Symbols

While dream symbols are often unique to the individual dreamer, there are certain categories of symbols that can be helpful when interpreting a dream. Within our culture there are many spiritually perverted ways to interpret these symbols, so it's critical to filter your understanding through the boundaries of God's Word and guidance when interpreting a dream that comes from Him. Some of the common categories of dream symbols include activities, tone, numbers, colors, people, names, and locations. These symbols can have both spiritual and literal significance depending on the context of the dream.

Activities

One of the most important symbols in dream interpretation is the main event that takes place in the dream. Dreams can be puzzling enough that we get in a habit of not paying proper attention to *what* happened. Merely dreaming about a snake, for instance, without considering the activity around it, can lead to a skewed interpretation. The difference between being bitten by a snake and killing a snake presents two vastly different meanings.

Let's return to Joseph. Both the cupbearer and the baker shared their dreams with him in Genesis 40. As previously shared, Joseph interpreted the cupbearer's dream and predicted his favorable future. But the baker's dream presented a less desirable future. The activity in both dreams provided insights into the fates of the individuals. In the cupbearer's dream, Joseph interpreted the activity of a vine producing ripe grapes. The cupbearer was portrayed holding the king's cup, pressing the grapes into the cup and returning it to the king's hands. This activity illustrated the restoration of the cupbearer's previous position.

The baker's dream told a different story. While carrying three baskets on his head, the baker saw that birds came and ate all the baked goods intended for the king. It's essential to observe the activity in this dream, which emphasizes the failure of the baked goods to make it to the king's table, instead being eaten by the birds. If the details of the birds' actions were ignored, the dream could be misinterpreted as one of restoration for the baker. But by taking the activity into account, it was clear that this was not a dream of revival, but rather an emphasis on termination. The baker was already in jail, but the dream went beyond that. When

Joseph interpreted the dream, the activity signified the baker's imminent death, ordered by the king.

Thus, in interpreting dreams, it is essential to pay attention to the actions and events that take place. By looking at the activity in detail, we can gain a more precise interpretation of the dream.

Tone

The overall tone of a dream can reveal the emotion behind the message, such as an ominous feeling signaling a warning, or hope and encouragement signaling favor and restoration. A symbol that is positive for one person could be negative for another, depending on the tone of the dream.

The tone of a dream has a significant impact on our understanding of it. For example, I had a dream where flying sharks suddenly emerged and devoured all the flies in the area. While I felt concerned about the sharks, I also experienced peace, knowing that I was protected from harm. This led me to consider the plagues in Egypt that affected only the Egyptians who opposed God's people. Yet God's people remained sheltered from the plagues.

Understanding the tone of the dream was essential in deciphering the message's depth. In this dream, there was an absence of flies, which naturally consume dead matter. Without flies in the world, there would be rubbish everywhere. The flies symbolized that which consumes the dead works in the lives of people. The Bible instructs us to repent from dead works, which are contrary to the ways of God.[5] With the flies extinct, such dead works would be evident to the world. The flying sharks represented the media, revealing hidden secrets and dead works to the public.

The dream conveyed a prophetic message about upcoming events, and the Holy Spirit revealed to me that certain media channels would expose individuals whose public image was a false representation of their true character. These wolves in sheep's clothing would be revealed, exposing the truth of their actions even though they believed them to be hidden from society. Understanding the tone gave insight into this message's purpose, resulting in a fuller comprehension of the prophetic meaning.

Another example is a dream a friend shared with me that initially alarmed her. She dreamed of an animal attacking her, and she was concerned when describing the dream's symbols. But when asked how she felt in the dream, she revealed a sense of calm and confidence, knowing she could either defeat or escape the animal. Understanding the dream's tone shifted the interpretation to suggest an upcoming obstacle in her waking life, but she should not fear because God would make a way for her. When we discerned the emotional tone in the dream, its meaning became clearer and allowed her to trust in God's provision and protection.

> A symbol that is positive for one person could be negative for another.

Whether it is a warning or an uplifting message, the tone is crucial in comprehending dream interpretations accurately.

Numbers

Numbers play an integral role in our understanding of the world around us. God established patterns of order and structure through numbers. For instance, in Genesis 2:2, we read, "And on the seventh day God ended His work which He had done, and He rested on the seventh day from all His work which He had done." We then see a numerical pattern and symbolism of the number seven representing completion or perfection.

Numbers are significant in God's communication with us, as they can be used as symbols to convey deeper spiritual truths. In the Bible, we see numerous examples of how God uses numbers to communicate His purposes and plans to His people. One example is the cupbearer's dream that Joseph interpreted, in which three branches represented three days until the cupbearer would be restored to his original position. Biblically, the number three represents completion as seen in the completeness of the Godhead (God the Father, the Son, and the Holy Spirit) as well as in Jesus's rising on the third day after His crucifixion.

Another significant number in the Bible is forty, which generally symbolizes a period of testing, trials, or preparation before a new beginning or significant change. This is seen in the forty years Moses spent in Egypt and again in the desert before leading God's people out of slavery, as well as in Jesus's forty-day fast in the wilderness before beginning His ministry.

As you study the Bible, you'll begin to discover that many numbers have distinctive patterns of meanings with God. A number may also represent a scripture that God wants you to hold on to as a reminder of His promise to you.

For instance, there was a time in my life when the Lord asked me to pray daily at 3:20 a.m. At first, I needed to set an alarm to wake up, but then I began waking naturally right after a dream, and when I looked at the clock, it was always 3:20 a.m.—just before my alarm went off. I didn't understand the significance of the time until I asked the Lord and He led me to Ephesians 3:20, which speaks to God's ability to do exceedingly and abundantly above all we could ask or think. This scripture encouraged me during a season when I felt that God's visions for my life were beyond what I could imagine. It reminded me to walk by faith and trust in the One who called me, and it remains one of my favorite scriptures to this day.

In addition to representing scriptures or spiritual insights, numbers can also have literal meanings in a dream. For example, I once heard a young lady's dream in which she was wrestling in a ring with three demonic-looking creatures. The Lord gave me a spiritual insight on the interpretation of the dream, that these creatures represented three people at her workplace who had been making her job difficult and making her feel as though she should quit. The reason why the three creatures looked demonic was because their attacks toward her were not random, but instead had an evil influence behind them. Such experiences remind us that "our struggle is not against flesh and blood, but against the rulers, against the authorities, against the powers of this dark world and against the spiritual forces of evil in the heavenly realms."[6]

It is clear that God communicates through numbers, and dreams can be a channel to receive His messages through the use of numbers. When numbers stand out in your dream, pay attention to them. This could be the number of objects, animals, or people in the dream; seeing a specific time in the dream; or constantly waking up at a specific time after a dream. These details are essential to understanding your dream.

However, it is critical not to fall into the trap of New Age doctrines such as "angel numbers." The idea behind angel numbers is that by repeatedly seeing certain number sequences, you are receiving divine guidance from an angel. This is often based on popular culture and not on biblical foundations. For example, the number 11:11 has become trendy, and people attribute its repeated appearance to divine intervention. But this may be more related to memory and familiarity rather than divine guidance. It's like when you desire a certain car, and then suddenly you see the car everywhere. Why? By default, your mind pays attention to what you are consciously familiar with or emotionally invested in. So seeing a certain number repeatedly does not necessarily indicate that it is a message from God. It is important to rely on the leading of the Holy Spirit to discern the meaning of numbers in your dreams.

Following angel numbers, or any external source outside of God, can lead to deception and manipulation by the Enemy. If you attribute meaning to a number that has no biblical foundation, you open yourself up to being misled because Satan is an angel whose mission is to deceive God's people. For instance, if a particular angel number is believed to indicate that you are on the right path, the Enemy can manipulate your attention toward that number to keep you on the wrong path. It is important to rely only on God's guidance and not on external sources that can lead you astray.

While numbers can be useful in interpreting dreams and discerning God's will, they should never take the place of a personal relationship with Him. As we seek to understand the symbolism and significance of numbers, we should first be seeking to grow closer to God and deeper in our understanding of His character.

Colors

A while back, a friend of mine was contemplating proposing to his girlfriend but had reservations about whether she was in line with God's will for his life. He knew that relying on his own wisdom or emotions would not be enough, having previously made that mistake. So he committed his request to prayer, seeking God's approval. God answered him through a dream. In this dream, he saw two versions of his life—one with his girlfriend and the other without her. The scenes without her were in black and white, and he was unhappy and unfulfilled. But the scenes with her were in color, vibrant and beautiful, and he was full of joy and gladness. Through prayer, he recognized that his dream was a clear sign from God, and my friend proposed, got married, and is now grateful for the woman God gave him.

Colors are a part of God's creation and reflect the beauty of His handiwork.

I remember a dream I had as a child when I was going through a time of sadness and longing for my absent father. I desired for him to lift me up and swing me around. In the dream, I experienced my first encounter with God the Father, and it was truly glorious. His essence radiated with a magnificence of light that rendered His face blinding to behold. I couldn't see it and kept my head down in awe. We were in a beautiful garden filled with radiant, colorful flowers that I had never seen before. The atmosphere was charged with an unexplainable joy that communicated itself to me. Then God did the unthinkable. He picked me up and began to swing me around, making me so happy that tears of joy streamed down my face. Even upon waking up, I was uplifted by the intense feeling of happiness and excitement. I realized that God truly is my heavenly Father, and though it may seem like something is missing in my natural life, that is not the case. Since that dream, my life has been greatly impacted, and recalling those indescribable colors and that experience always brings a smile to my face.

The vibrancy of colors in dreams can be highly symbolic and capture the emotions or messages being conveyed. The dream I had of God swinging me around had such brilliant colors that infused the message with joy and excitement.

Colors in dreams can sometimes act as signs that confirm what you are meant to do in your waking life. For example, if you are sharing a message with someone in a dream, and their outfit's color stands out to you, and then later, when you see them in real life, they are indeed dressed in that particular color, it can be a confirmation that you should proceed with sharing the message of the dream.

People

One of the most challenging obstacles in dream interpretation is when people are featured in the dream. It is easy to assume that the dream only has a literal meaning, but it is often loaded with spiritual significance. This can create confusion in some instances.

For example, a young lady had a dream in which I brought correction to her and explained why her actions were not pleasing to God. When she repented, she would receive a breakthrough for what she had been praying for. She applied the message and witnessed significant shifts in her life. When she shared her experience with me, she interpreted it as a sign that I was supposed to personally mentor her, which wasn't a possibility at the time. Mentorship doesn't always require a personal relationship, but rather the ability to learn from someone else's teachings. I commit the decision to mentor someone personally to the Lord. But in this case, I sensed that it was not about mentorship. Rather, because she looked up to me spiritually, God could use my likeness in her dream to communicate a message to her. I have had similar experiences with my pastor because I recognize his spiritual authority. It is not uncommon for people to see their natural parents used in this manner.

In dreams, people can be used as symbols that communicate a specific message from God. For instance, a dream might reference someone's name or something essential about their lives that is significant to the message God is communicating to you. Before meeting my husband, I had several symbolic dreams regarding key things about him. But these dreams weren't meant to cause obsession or lead me to conclude that a specific person was my future spouse. Instead, these dreams were there to serve as a confirmation that I would meet the person God ordained for me.

These dreams taught me that some dreams, especially those involving people, may take time to interpret, as their message may not be applicable to the present situation, but rather a confirmation for something in the future. Indeed, dreams can serve as a powerful reminder that God will guide and lead us through life's many transitions. But interpreting these dreams might require patience and a trustful dependence on the Holy Spirit for guidance.

Then there's the complexity around cultural background and beliefs on what it means to dream about dead people. Some may view it as good while others see it as a bad thing, but it's not so simple. Biblically, we are cautioned against consulting the dead,[7] which is an abomination to God. People may justify interpreting dreams about the dead as negative or evil, but it's worth noting that dreaming about the dead is not the same as consulting them. Consulting refers to seeking out information or advice, while in dreams, the dead may appear to be coming to us.

The transfiguration scene in Luke 9 during Jesus's time on earth sheds some light on this topic. Jesus took three of His disciples on a mountainside to pray, and while He was praying, He transformed, and His face shone like the sun, and even His clothes became pure white.[8] Moses and Elijah appeared in heavenly glory, and they conversed with Jesus. Though the disciples were asleep during this event, they awoke to see Jesus transfigured and the two men speaking to Him. While the Bible doesn't specify how the disciples made this identification, divine insight allowed Peter to recognize them as Moses and Elijah.

Many people who dream of dead loved ones experience a common feeling of being able to communicate without words, an understanding of their presence that goes beyond verbal dialogue. We tend to see our loved ones in a radiant way in such dreams, regardless of how they passed. Sometimes they appear younger or healthier. Emotionally, the tone is peaceful, comforting, and even joyous.

Such dreams can come from God and are often used by Him to encourage us about our loved ones' eternal destinies. For example, if they died tragically or in pain, dreaming about them in a pain-free and joyous state can bring us comfort. When we view life from an eternal perspective, we gain knowledge that death is not final and that our deceased loved ones have transitioned from the earthly realm to the spiritual realm. These encounters might not involve touching or speaking with our deceased loved ones, but seeing them in dreams from God is possible.

These dreams could also come as warning dreams. In scenarios where a person who is dead is instructing you to follow them, or is driving a car and you're in the passenger seat, it can leave you with an eerie feeling, because in such dreams the dead individual represents the spirit of death and should be prayed against upon waking up.

It's important to note that dreams coming from Satan can also involve dead people, but as we discussed in a previous chapter, you can identify the source of such dreams by the nature it embodies. If you wake up fearful or anxious, don't give in to the temptation to come into agreement with the narrative of fear or torment. Take inventory of your soul's intake, and shut any doors to things that allowed access for Satan to manipulate your dreams.

Here are a few examples of how people we know might show up in our dreams, and general insights into their meanings:

- *Negative Events Happening to Someone You Know:* Such dreams might be watchman dreams, indicating the need for prayer. This could prompt you to intercede on behalf of the person you dreamed about.

- *Involving a Spiritual Leader:* A dream portraying a spiritual leader in a positive manner may signify God's use of the image to communicate a message to you, given that person's spiritual authority in your life. A dream portraying a spiritual leader in a harmful way may serve as a warning dream, suggesting that the leader might align with what Jesus refers to as wolves in sheep's clothing.[9] This could be an indication to reconsider being under their ministry.

- *Revealing Someone You Know as a Source of Potential Danger:* This type of dream could be a warning, urging you to be cautious or avoid certain situations related to that person.

- *Romantic Interest Shown in a Negative Light:* This may be a warning dream, revealing hidden traits that signal a red flag. Pay attention to such dreams to make informed decisions and avoid unnecessary hurt.

- *Romantic Interest as Your Spouse:* If you're not actively dating the person, this dream could originate from your own desires. Evaluate the fruit it produces—if it leads to an unhealthy obsession or attributes inconsistent with God's character, it may not be a God dream at all. But if you're actively dating the person, it could serve as confirmation, especially if you've been seeking God's guidance in prayer about the possibility of marriage.

- *Someone You Know in a Symbolic Manner:* In a dream where someone you know appears in a seemingly random placement, it may not necessarily be about the person but could carry symbolic significance. For instance, I once had a dream where I had supernatural abilities to protect myself and others from a mass shooter. Among the various people in the dream, my friend Nina stood out right before the incident happened. Researching her name, I discovered that Nina means grace. This added another layer of meaning to the dream as it resonated with the scripture, "My grace is sufficient for you."[10] Grace, in this context, refers to divine empowerment from God, enabling us to achieve what would be impossible in our own strength. The dream's message was a reminder that God had endowed me with His grace to stand against the Enemy.

Names

Names and phrases can emphasize the connection between the message of the dream and the individual being named. Depending on how the name is used or seen, it could highlight different meanings. For example, if someone is called by a name that is not their given name, the meaning of that name might be critical to the message God is communicating to them.

In some cases, the message of the dream might be either hidden or emphasized through the use of a name or a phrase, providing confirmation that the dream came from God. These types of dreams go beyond what an individual's mind could create, making them more surreal and powerful, underscoring the unique nature of the message.

I recently had a dream where I was transformed from a farmer into a warrior after an encounter with a man named Igor who put a sword in my hand and called me a warrior. Curious about the meaning of this encounter, I researched the name *Igor* and discovered that it is a male name of Russian origin that means "warrior." As I prayed and meditated on the symbols in the dream, I realized that this encounter was a call to step into a new season of my life.

In the dream, my transformation from a farmer to a warrior highlighted the importance of protecting and defending what I had sown and cultivated from those who would seek to harm it. Just as a seed must first be hidden underground before it can grow and bear fruit, I had been diligently working behind the scenes, and now it was time to protect the fruit of my labor. The use of the name *Igor* in the dream was a confirmation that God was indeed calling me to be a warrior, to defend and protect the harvest of my prayers and hard work. Here are some practical tips on what to do if you hear or see a name in your dream:

1. *Pray for guidance.* Ask God for clarity and understanding regarding the symbolism and the specific role or message associated with the name in your dream.

2. *Research the meaning.* Names often carry significant meanings and can provide valuable insights into the message God might be sending.

3. *Explore biblical significance.* Consider if the name has any biblical significance. Many names in the Bible hold specific meanings or are associated with certain qualities.

4. *Reflect on personal associations.* Sometimes the significance might be tied to your unique experiences or relationships.

5. *Consider symbolic connections.* Names and phrases can have symbolic connections to your current circumstances or future endeavors. In the example of the dream

where I learned the name *Igor*, the symbolism was connected to my own experience of stepping into a new season of life.

Locations

The setting of a dream can reveal valuable insight into the dream's underlying message. For example, being in a desert could represent a period of spiritual testing, while being in a garden might symbolize a place of rest.

When analyzing the location in a dream, it's important to note whether it's a familiar or unfamiliar place. For instance, if God is warning you of a potential setback due to your decisions, you might dream of being back in your old high school or university and failing an exam. Alternatively, if you dream of taking a test in a school location, it might be a message highlighting a challenge you're currently facing in your waking life, indicating that your handling of the situation is crucial to stepping into the next season of your life.

Dreams that take place in unfamiliar locations may hold significant meaning that will be revealed later.

After my father was tragically murdered, my mother discovered that he had acquired several plots of land during his lifetime. While she had the documentation for a specific parcel, its exact location remained unknown. Certain family members, motivated by greed, withheld crucial information, complicating efforts to locate the land.

For nearly two decades, my mother experienced recurring dreams centered around a particular setting—land near a body of water. Although each dream brought new details, the location remained a mystery. The significance of these dreams eluded us until a gentleman, privy to this information, informed my mother. As he described the land as being by a body of water, my mother broke down in tears, realizing that indeed this was the land. It was located in my father's hometown, and we decided to build a home on it in his honor.

God utilized my mother's recurring dream as a constant reminder that restoration was forthcoming. Although we were unaware of the significance of the dream at the time, we persevered in prayer, trusting that God's will would be manifested. And indeed, it was. The revelation of the land strengthened our faith by reminding us that even when we don't see it, God is always working for our good. When you pay close attention to the location in your dreams, it could uncover significant meanings that you may need to understand presently or in the future.

Dream interpretation requires understanding dream symbols. But interpreting the symbols themselves is not always straightforward. Here are some practical truths to help activate the gift of dream interpretation.

You Have the Gift

As a believer in Jesus Christ, you have the gift of interpreting dreams through the Holy Spirit. The Spirit of the Lord is the interpreter, enabling us to understand the messages our dreams convey.

Although we have received the Holy Spirit[11] and, with it, the gift of dream interpretation, we must make room in our lives to exercise the gift. According to 1 Corinthians 2:11, only the Spirit of God knows God's mind. When you have dreams from God with symbols unique to the message He's conveying, His Spirit helps you understand.

Keep It in God's Presence

Keeping dream interpretation in God's presence is essential. Relying on internet research sites for dream interpretation may mislead you about the message of your dream. But as some symbols in a dream may have a literal meaning, researching to understand the natural characteristics of a symbol does no harm.

For instance, in my dream about flies, understanding the natural outcome of what would happen on earth if flies became extinct deepened my understanding of the dream. Similarly, researching the meaning of a name or the existence of a location can increase understanding and capacity for the Holy Spirit to reveal the dream's meaning. Sometimes I might hear a word I've never heard before, but upon researching its meaning, the meaning of the word connects to God's message for me through the dream. Nevertheless, we must be mindful that relying on sources outside of the One who sent the dream for spiritual meaning can be misleading.

Scripture teaches us about different angels and their functions, one of whom is the angel Gabriel, who carried divine revelation and deep insight. God sent him to deliver important messages, such as to Zechariah about his wife bearing a child even though she was previously barren. Gabriel's response to

Zechariah's doubts was, "I am Gabriel. I stand in the presence of God,"[12] emphasizing that his words came from God's presence.

We should take this posture and keep dream interpretation in God's presence. Writing down and identifying symbols in our dreams, and presenting those to God in worship and prayer can help us understand the messages He's conveying. While researching natural meanings of symbols, we should not rely on our understanding but present our thoughts to the Holy Spirit and pay attention to the direction His peace leads us as it relates to understanding the dream, the thoughts that come up, and the promptings that come to us. This is how we exercise dream interpretation with the Holy Spirit.

Continue the Conversation in Prayer

It's essential to view our prayer time not as a religious practice to receive dream interpretations but as a way of continuing the conversation with God. Imagining the dream as if it's Jesus's walking into your room to speak with you will help you understand the significance of the messages conveyed through the dream channel. The communication between you and God can be conversational. Speaking with God and waiting to receive His response can deepen your understanding of His message and intent.

Often, we treat prayer as a one-sided conversation, concluding with "In Jesus's name, amen," and move on with our day. We allow life's distractions to creep in and then wonder why we haven't heard from God. Imagine attending a therapy session just to speak and then leave. The effectiveness of therapy comes from the dialogue and intentional setting shared between you and the therapist, with no outside distractions. Shouldn't this be the case for our communication with God? Does He have our undivided attention during moments of prayer and worship?

Our relationship with God allows us to speak to Him anywhere, at any time, but how we lay the foundation at the beginning of our day matters. It reveals our reverence and respect for His presence and His word to us. When we prioritize Him, giving Him our full attention during the time allocated for prayer, the conversation will continue, and further insight about our dreams can be made clear to us, either in that moment or later.

Questions for Interpretation

Proverbs 25:2 says, "It is the glory of God to conceal a matter, but the glory of kings is to search out a matter." This verse reminds us of the positioning of authority, honor, and favor that we step into when we align ourselves with God's will and Word. But the scripture says we must "search out a matter." This searching requires humility through presenting the dream before God. In doing so, our wisdom is submitted to the wisdom of God, and we receive His guidance on how to apply the dream's meaning in our lives.

After waking, pause to write down what you can remember of your dream, and pray for God to reveal the meaning to you. Then take some time to reflect on these questions, both within yourself and in communion with God, as you seek the meaning of the dream.

- What was the activity and the tone of the dream?

- Is this a recurring dream? Recurring dreams tend to emphasize that either the dream is yet to be properly understood, and God is sending the same message again, or the dream holds deep truths to be understood at a future time, and God is using the dream symbols as a reminder.

- What do the symbols mean individually, and do they have literal or biblical meanings?

- What do the symbols mean collectively? Together, what kind of story do they tell?

- Based on the symbols used in the dream, does the message represent the nature of God, of Satan, or of self? If you identify the source as God, pay close attention to the remaining questions.

- What kind of dream is this? Is it a directional dream, impartation dream, strategy dream, encouragement dream, warning dream, or watchman dream?

- Putting it all together, what's the primary message of the dream?

Sometimes the message of a dream is not meant to be understood immediately, but it's a confirmation of a future event. When the message of the dream seems unclear, it's essential to keep the dream in front of you and revisit the details regularly because, with time, the dream's message can become clearer.

Trusted Counsel

Interpreting dreams, particularly when the messages seem disruptive, requires caution. Jumping to the conclusion that a message is from God and being quick to say, "God said" or "God told me" is risky. To safeguard against potential deception or misunderstanding, seek additional insight from trusted people of faith.

The people you seek feedback and advice from should be two or three individuals in your life who deeply love and revere God. They should possess godly wisdom and not be influenced by their emotions. Trusted counsel can listen to your interpretation and evaluate its consistency with the nature of God, pray with you for clarity, and provide confirmation or a different perspective on its meaning. Their primary concern is pleasing God rather than simply agreeing with or pleasing you.

If you don't have such individuals in your life right now, take heart, because God has unexpected ways of confirming whether the dream came from Him, due to the gravity of its message. For example, perhaps you receive a call from someone out of the blue who suggests the exact message you received in your dream. When lacking trusted counsel, you can pray to the Lord for help in discovering a church community where you can connect and get involved. Joining a small group or volunteering in a team within the church can help you build strong faith communities. In fact, serving in the church has allowed me to develop some of my closest and most trusted friendships.

I have encountered numerous instances where people misinterpret their dreams. They often cherry-pick parts of a biblical figure's story to validate their interpretation.

For instance, let's consider a young lady who had a dream

about seeing herself in a different city. Immediately, she interpreted it as a divine call, paralleling Abraham's journey to trust God and leave everything behind. She believed she should move to the city with no money, no place to live, and no contacts. When her friends and family questioned her decision, she became defensive, dismissing their concerns as a lack of understanding of God's calling in her life. She embarked on the journey, but when things didn't unfold as she expected, she placed blame on God and carried bitterness in her heart. This situation might have unfolded differently if she had sought counsel from someone who could have highlighted the flaws in her interpretation. Through prayer and guidance, they could have helped her take the time to interpret the symbolic elements of her dream with wisdom and discernment.

Romans 12:3 reminds us to have humility and not think too highly of ourselves. Thinking we are the wisest individuals can lead to disastrous outcomes. Despite my experience in interpreting dreams with God, there are certain dreams that I choose to share with trusted counsel before taking any action. This practice helps me gain valuable insights and discernment from others who may offer a different perspective, ask good questions, or provide guidance that I might have overlooked. It serves as a safeguard, ensuring that my interpretations are not solely based on my own understanding but are also aligned with wisdom and insight from others who deeply revere God.

It is important to be kind to yourself and not get discouraged when you misinterpret a dream. When you desire to understand your dreams to accurately and humbly comprehend the messages God has for you, your heart opens to the truth, which sharpens your sensitivity to recognize His voice. Discerning God's voice is a process that requires dying to oneself to avoid personal emotions interfering with His message. God is patient with us, so let us extend the same patience to ourselves.

Heavenly Father, thank You for Your Holy Spirit who enables me to interpret my dreams as I humble myself to Your leading. Help me to let go of personal biases and emotions that may interfere with understanding Your message to me. I place my trust in You, knowing that Your wisdom surpasses our understanding. Lead me as I navigate the intricate landscape of my dreams, and help me interpret them in alignment with Your truth. In Jesus's name, amen.

Reflection Questions

1. Think back to a dream you've had. What symbols stand out to you now, and how do they affirm or shift your understanding of the dream's message?

2. What question from the list on pages 125–26 might you include in your prayers today to seek God's guidance in comprehending your dreams better?

PART III

Hello Dreamer,

At this point, you may notice that the person who began this journey is not the same person reading this page. I am proud of your commitment and diligence in knowing the power of your dreams.

Dreams are not merely a means to an end. When they are from God, they bring us into better alignment with Him, give us a deeper understanding of His will, and equip us to live out the purpose He has designed for our lives. Nurturing this connection involves delving into the significance of God's word in our lives. Together, we will explore how to receive more through our dreams, embracing a life that is truly empowered by the insights gleaned from the realm of dreams.

So, let's tap in!

Yours truly,
Stephanie

SEVEN

THE POWER OF
GOD'S WORD

Before I formed you in the womb I knew you.

—Jeremiah 1:5, ESV

I n 2014, I watched a movie called *Heaven Is for Real.* It's based on the true story of Colton Burpo, who visited heaven during a near-death experience at age four while undergoing surgery for his burst appendix. During the encounter, Colton met his unborn sister, whom his mother miscarried a year prior to his birth. What's even more interesting is that he had never been told about this sister.

There was no doubt in my mind about the truth of his experience because I had also had supernatural encounters starting when I was just nine years old. In one of those encounters, I visited heaven and, for a moment, I saw the children I will give birth to. Seeing them, I understood that these were kids assigned to my life because of the unique plans and purposes God has for them, which align with the environment and experiences they will have as my children. I later had other encounters where I was given certain key details about who they'll be.

Fast-forward to when I met my husband, and we would have conversations where he shared details with me regarding what God had revealed to him about the children he would have. It was like he had read a page from my journal where I had recorded what God had shown me. These details are important because they point to the truth that our lives didn't start here. They show that the reason there's a heaven for us to return to and in some cases visit is because we didn't just start on earth. For us, heaven is not just a location but a reality proclaiming that our beginning started with God.

As we embrace this truth, we must also acknowledge that it is our reliance on God that keeps us walking on the path He intended for us. Proverbs 14:12 serves as a poignant reminder, stating, "There is a way that seems right to a man, but its end is the way of death." It is crucial for us to remain vigilant and not become complacent with the praise of others regarding our wisdom, intellect, or gifts. Such exaltation can seduce us into paths that were never intended for us to walk.

In learning to discern God's voice in our dreams, we must understand why we need His Word in our lives. While we have already acknowledged that God speaks to us, let us explore further why His Word is so indispensable in our lives.

> How can you rely solely on your wisdom when you did not give yourself life?

Contrary to cultural trends about what it means to walk in "your truth," your truth is not limited to the guidance of your wisdom about who you are. How can you rely solely on your wisdom when you did not give yourself life? Your life started with the breath of God and was designed to be lived in partnership with God, not only to discover the uniqueness of the assignment on your life but also to ensure you fulfill it. God is there to guide you through the hurt, betrayals, confusion, relationships, excitement, and transitions that come with living. His Word provides navigation for your destiny so that, no matter life's detours, He can reroute you.

During a supernatural encounter, God revealed to the prophet Jeremiah his identity and purpose. Jeremiah initially struggled with the contradiction of the truth of God's words and how he perceived himself. Nevertheless, God set the tone in the conversation with Jeremiah by first saying, "Before I formed you in the womb I knew you; before you were born I sanctified you; I ordained you a prophet to the nations."[1] In other words, "Before you started on earth, before your mother discovered she was pregnant with you, and before your parents met, you were known. Neither the timing of your birth nor the family you were born into was an accident. You see, Jeremiah, it wasn't the fertilization of an egg that started your journey. It started with Me."

The same is true for you. God formed you in your mother's womb. He placed you there because your life was appointed for the generation, the community, and the family you were born into. You are known by God, you were sent here for an ordained purpose that breaks the limitations of your perceived ability, and you were made to hear His voice as the guide for your life.

God Appointed You

There is a captivating story in 1 Kings 17 about the prophet Elijah and a widow. Elijah was a powerful prophet of God during a period of drought in the land. By God's direction, Elijah declared the drought as a rebuke to the people's divided worship, as some followed God, others idolized the false god Baal, and some even engaged in both. The drought served to confront their false beliefs and demonstrate that only the Lord God Almighty deserves true worship. Elijah predicted a three-and-a-half-year drought, which came to pass. But during this time, God miraculously met Elijah's needs. God directed him to a specific location with water and commanded ravens to miraculously provide food for him. When the supernatural water supply dried up, God redirected Elijah to a town where a widow had been *commanded* to provide for him.

One might expect, based on God's "command," that the widow would have had a secret supply of food and that God had already spoken to her about Elijah's visit. But that was not the case. When Elijah met the widow and humbly requested some food from her, she hesitated. She told him that she and her son were down to their last bit of food and were preparing their final meal before succumbing to starvation. This might make us question what God meant when He informed Elijah, "I have commanded a widow there to provide for you."[2] Did the widow not hear God's command?

To understand this, we need to explore the meaning of the word *command.* In this context, the word can be translated as "appoint" or "ordain."[3] It is the same meaning for the word used by God when speaking to the prophet Jeremiah, revealing that even before Jeremiah's birth, he was appointed and ordained to be a prophet.[4] The purpose for his life could only be fulfilled after it was revealed to Jeremiah.

There are specific purposes assigned to your life. When God

reveals these assignments to you, you can then step into and live out His will for your life.

In the story of Elijah and the widow, we see how the widow aligned herself with God's truth about her when Elijah revealed the word of God to her. Then, through her obedience, she experienced supernatural provision that spared both her and her son during the famine.

Elijah, as a prophet, represented someone who declared God's wisdom and guidance. In those times, prophets were relied upon to speak God's word since the Holy Spirit did not yet dwell within all believers as He does today. But now that the Holy Spirit has been released to all who accept Jesus, each of us can personally receive God's word in order to align ourselves with who He has appointed us to be.

The widow wasn't chosen randomly; she was appointed by God. Though she was initially fearful, God's word turned her circumstances around. Just as the word of God revealed to the widow what she was appointed by God to do, it will do the same for you.

God's Word Reveals

In the beginning God created the heavens and the earth. The earth was without form, and void; and darkness was on the face of the deep. And the Spirit of God was hovering over the face of the waters. Then God said, "Let there be light"; and there was light.[5]

The historical account of creation teaches us a very valuable pattern about God: His word reveals the intent of His creation.

"Let there be" is from the Hebrew translation *hāyâ,* which means "appear."[6] In other words, "Let there be light" can be better understood as "Light, appear" or "Light, reveal yourself." But if the saying is true that darkness is merely the absence of light, then it's possible that light wasn't hidden in darkness, but in the word of God.

The revealing of the intent of creation was triggered by His word, and in the same way, the revealing of who you truly are is also accessed through His word.

When my mother was pregnant with my older brother, she received a prophetic word from a pastor that the child she was carrying would be used greatly by God and that he would have a sister who would come shortly after him. The pastor explained that my brother and I would have a unique bond and that I would also teach God's Word.

My birth happened just as the pastor said, but when I encountered God at nine years old and was building a personal relationship with Him, I didn't desire to be a Bible teacher or a pastor. I wanted to pursue a career in law and have a talk show. As I got older, I ended up studying mass communication in college and began doing interviews with different celebrities for a digital show I started called *Voice of Hope.* I then got into real estate, flipping homes with my brother.

One day I woke up feeling disconnected from myself. I felt unsettled and couldn't shake off the feeling for days, which then turned into weeks. On the surface, everything was great. I was making great money. On paper, I had everything I needed to be happy, but I wasn't. It felt like I wasn't living the life that was authentic to my identity. To get clarity from God about my life and purpose, I decided to fast. During the fast, through a series of dreams and other means of confirmation, alongside vetting my interpretations with trusted counsel, God's voice instructed me to walk away from the real estate business and attend ONE, A Potter's House Church. The first time I walked into the church, I received a word from God that said, "In this house, I will raise you as a minister of the gospel."

What's so interesting about this is that I don't come from a family of preachers, I didn't go to seminary, and at the time I didn't have a personal relationship with the pastors or leaders of the church. So, to hear that I would be a pastor in this church sounded out of reach. Still, I did as God directed and started attending. Then I had a dream in which I saw myself serving as an usher in the church. Ushers are the people in the church who welcome you when you arrive, help you find a seat, walk around the aisles to offer tissues when needed, and provide any other assistance or help with the flow of the church service.

When I woke up from this dream, I knew I had received a word from God instructing me to volunteer in the church as an usher. The moment I made that decision, He continued to speak, and I understood that while serving as an usher, I should never miss a service during that year and that volunteering should be my sole focus.

I obeyed this instruction and lived off my savings during that time. It was a very difficult year of my life and not everyone understood my decision. My family was both confused and upset with me because they believed I was jeopardizing my future. They were familiar with seeing me make decisions based on God's guidance, which had never let me down before. But this time, my choice seemed too unsettling for them and they were genuinely concerned for my well-being, desiring for me to be established instead of walking away from a thriving career. Even though I knew I was obeying God, this season of my life had its ups and downs. Nevertheless, what others perceived to be darkness and without form was light to me. I knew I was where I needed to be. I felt connected to God's purpose while serving as an usher.

Little did I know that the way the word of God revealed that I should serve in the church is the same way God's word came to my pastor to have me preach in the church. Eventually God would also direct my pastor to ask me to become the campus pastor and later the executive pastor. It's crazy to think that before I was conceived, I was known, and that it was always in the plans of God that I would be the pastor I am—one who is committed to helping people understand the power of relationship with God.

I would have never taken this journey in my own wisdom, but this truth that was foreknown by God became my reality. I'm working on projects and excelling in industries that I have no natural qualification or experience in because of the power of God's word to continually reveal the eternal me—the me that was known before I was born, and the me I will continue to discover through His word.

The awareness of your truest self isn't found backpacking through Europe or going on a mission trip. Although these activities can be fun and enlightening, your true self is discovered and revealed through the word of God. So, embracing the messages from God through your dreams, and the many ways He speaks, becomes a powerful pathway to understanding and unlocking the profound truths that shape your life.

God's Word Establishes

In 2023, I had the incredible opportunity to preach at and attend VOUSCon, a conference in Miami led by two pastors I deeply admire, Rich and DawnCheré Wilkerson. At one point during the conference, I had a unique experience in a one-on-one session with hundreds of people present. Building upon the teaching I had shared earlier that day, I opened the floor for questions and discussion.

To my expectation, the questions took a divine turn as we delved into the topic. I felt led by the Holy Spirit to shift our focus toward prayer for healing. A sense of urgency filled the room as we collectively prayed for God's healing power to manifest in the lives of those who were facing physical ailments. In that moment of prayer, I sensed the Holy Spirit guiding me to invite anyone in need of physical healing to come forward. It became clear that God wanted to demonstrate His healing nature and the power of His presence to all those in attendance.

It was a powerful and transformative experience as individuals stepped forward, seeking God's touch and displaying their faith in His ability to heal. This moment served as a testimony to the truth that, indeed, God is a healer, capable of working miracles in our lives.

It was a divine moment orchestrated by God, not only for the purpose of healing but also for building and strengthening the faith of those present. The undeniable presence of God's healing power filled the room.

Among those who came forward was an older woman in a wheelchair, fervently believing in God's ability to restore strength to her legs. As I placed my hands on her legs and began to pray,

I received a clear instruction from the Lord: "Have her stand up and walk." Although there could have been risks involved in following this instruction, I trusted in the word from God and enlisted the help of others to assist her in standing. With faith and anticipation, I encouraged her to take seven steps, assuring her that despite feeling shaky, she would not fall. As she began to walk, her legs initially exhibited instability, but I instructed those around her not to stand behind her, assuring them that she would not stumble.

To everyone's awe and amazement, her legs grew stronger and stronger with each step she took. Those who had accompanied her were overwhelmed with tears of joy, witnessing a miracle unfold before their eyes. They exclaimed that they had never seen her walk like that before.

In that moment, despite feeling a bit nervous, I rested my confidence solely in the word of God, for when His word is spoken, everything aligns to fulfill the purpose for which it was sent. As Isaiah 55:11 declares, "So shall My word be that goes forth from My mouth; it shall not return to Me void, but it shall accomplish what I please, and it shall prosper in the thing for which I sent it."

Jesus is described as the Word made flesh in John 1:14. This concept can be difficult for the human mind to fully grasp. But it signifies that, just as air exists even though it cannot be seen, words hold a spiritual dynamic. While words themselves may not be visible, they possess power and influence. Similarly, just as water vapor in the air can undergo condensation to transform into a tangible, liquid form, the concept of the Word becoming flesh represents the embodiment of Jesus as a person.

Jesus goes beyond being just any word. He is the Word through whom all things were created.[7] All of creation responds to Him as its source and sustainer. When a word is revealed, it carries the weight of establishing its intended purpose as we put it to action.

Remember Madam C. J. Walker? There's more to her story. She is recorded as the first female self-made millionaire in America in the *Guinness Book of World Records.* Since she was the first person in her family to be born free from slavery, her success didn't just pave the way for African American women; it spoke volumes of inspiration to women everywhere.

As we learned earlier, the story behind her success began with the inspiration to create hair products after experiencing severe hair loss due to a scalp infection, but the secret behind finding the formula to grow her hair came to her in a dream. She once explained her dream, saying, "God answered my prayer, for one night I had a dream, and in that dream a big black man appeared to me and told me what to mix up for my hair. Some of the remedy was grown in Africa, but I sent for it, mixed it, put it on my scalp, and in a few weeks my hair was coming in faster than it had ever fallen out. I tried it on my friends; it helped them. I made up my mind I would begin to sell it."[8]

> When God speaks, it's a transfer of knowledge for the benefit of the receiver and those who will be impacted by the outcome.

Madame C. J. Walker received a strategy dream, and by acting upon the insights from that dream, she set the stage for the fulfillment of its intended purpose.

When God, who knows everything, decides to tell you anything, it's to reveal and establish His purpose for and through your life. Deuteronomy 29:29 says, "The secret things belong to the LORD our God, but those things which are revealed belong to us and to our children forever." When God speaks, it's a transfer of knowledge for the benefit of the receiver and those who will be impacted by the outcome.

Madam C. J. Walker's life was plagued by many barriers. She was a daughter of former slaves, orphaned at the age of seven, married at fourteen, a mother at seventeen, and a widow at twenty.[9] Nevertheless, when the word of God came to her in a dream, it became her competitive advantage. As you act in alignment with God's revealed word to you, your purpose will come alive, you'll gain revelation for the solutions to the very problems that frustrated you, your life won't be aimless or limited by life's circumstances, and you'll live with precision, clarity, and strategy.

As you continue through this book and apply its teachings, your spiritual sensitivity will grow. You'll become more attuned to receiving His word for guidance and direction, uncovering your true identity and understanding the unique contributions you were designed to offer the world.

Heavenly Father, thank You for the wisdom found in Your revealed word. I acknowledge that the power of my dreams is intricately linked to the power of Your word unveiled through them. Grant me the strength and discernment to act in accordance with Your guidance, even in the face of perceived challenges or obstacles. May I walk confidently in the direction of Your word, trusting that with every step, there is provision and access to the purposes You have ordained for me. Illuminate my path, as I strive to align my actions with Your truths. In Jesus's name, amen.

Reflection Questions

1. What does it mean to you that you were made by God to hear His voice and His word? How does this challenge your perception of your own limitations? How does it encourage you?

2. Reflect on areas of your life where obedience to God's word may be lacking. Reflect and pray about why this might be.

EIGHT

ACCESS THROUGH FAITH

Whatever you ask in prayer, you
will receive, if you have faith.

—Matthew 21:22, ESV

While I was pregnant with my daughter Ariel, a few months after the pain from the fibroids miraculously disappeared, that same issue resurfaced. I fervently prayed for healing, for relief, yet nothing seemed to change. I felt confused and, to some extent, abandoned by God. Where was the God who had performed incredible miracles in and through my life? Yet despite my dwindling hope, I knew I could only turn to Him for help.

During a particularly overwhelming day, I reached out to my cousin who is not only a doctor but also a woman of faith. I asked her to join me in prayer, and that night, something extraordinary occurred. I had a profound encounter with the Lord Jesus in a dream, where He taught me His Word on the power of faith and prayer for healing. He revealed to me that my lack of faith was hindering the manifestation of my desired healing. I realized that, in truth, my faith extended only as far as believing that God would assist me in getting a restful night's sleep, which I achieved on that particular night. But I lacked the necessary faith to believe for complete healing of my ailment.

In His loving and compassionate manner, the Lord did not judge or treat me condescendingly. Instead, He showed me how He meets us at the level of our faith. He reminded me of instances in Scripture where people were healed as a result of their unwavering faith.[1] It became clear to me that I needed to develop my understanding in this area.

Upon waking, I earnestly asked the Lord to reveal to me how my lack of faith was evident. I felt compelled to call my cousin and share the encounter with her. As I recounted the events, I realized something crucial: Right after we had prayed, before lying down, I had exclaimed, "God, why won't You heal me?"

Hearing those words, my cousin repeated the same words the Lord Jesus spoke to me in the dream: "You don't have faith." I was taken aback, as I hadn't fully grasped the weight of my own admission.

She then posed a simple yet profound question: "What is faith?"

My response drew from Hebrews 11:1: "Now faith is the substance of things hoped for, the evidence of things not seen." As I spoke these words, a revelation washed over me. I realized that if I truly possessed faith, I would have spoken words of unwavering belief after our prayer. Instead, my words reflected doubt, undermining the evidence of a faithful God who could indeed heal me as promised in His Word.

After concluding my conversation with my cousin, I approached the study of God's Word with fresh eyes and a newfound perspective. I delved into passages that spoke directly about faith, particularly focusing on how the prayer of faith can bring healing to the sick.[2] As I immersed myself in these verses, the truth of God's Word resonated within me, solidifying my belief that He would indeed heal me, whether it be an immediate or a gradual process.

With renewed hope, I made a decision. Originally, I had planned to skip attending church service that Sunday due to my discomfort. But an inspired thought challenged me: *What would a healed me do? I would attend church service.* Determined, I pushed through my discomfort and made my way to church the following day. As I stepped into the sanctuary, a tangible presence of God's healing power enveloped me. In that sacred moment, I experienced a divine touch that utterly transformed my ailment. From that day forward, I never had to endure that same struggle again.

I accessed my healing through faith.

Faith is integral to accessing God's gifts. When we put our trust in God and believe in His promises, we open ourselves up to receiving the blessings that He has in store for us. Whether it's healing or dreaming with God, it all starts with faith, which is a steadfast confidence that God is faithful and will deliver on His promises.

I pray that your mind opens to the boundless possibilities that exist with God. Start believing that there are great encounters awaiting you in your life and in your dreams. I hold faith that what once seemed impossible to you will become possible—that you will have "walking on water" moments.

Walk on Water

Matthew 14 tells the well-known and captivating story of how Peter learned the power of faith to achieve the impossible. Peter and the other disciples, following Jesus's instruction, had set out in their boat after witnessing Him miraculously feed over five thousand people with just five loaves of bread and two fish. As they sailed, likely still in awe of the previous miracle, little did they know they were on the verge of witnessing Jesus defy expectations once more as He approached their boat, walking on water.

> Praying with faith goes beyond rational thought.

When the disciples saw Jesus walking on water, they did what was expected: "Ahhhh!" I'm not sure how long their scream lasted, but Scripture tells us "they cried out for fear."[3] Jesus calmed their anxieties by confirming to them that indeed it was Him. And then Peter prayed.

He said, "Lord, if it is You, command me to come to You on the water."[4] At this moment, all rational thought went out the window.

Praying with faith goes beyond rational thought. Our requests and expectations rise to the level of possibilities of the One we are speaking to. Peter's response to Jesus serves as a demonstration of faith through prayer. Peter was withdrawn from his five natural senses. He didn't need to walk on water to know it was Jesus, but he had come into a divine reasoning to recognize that if Jesus could walk on water, then *so could he.* Later Jesus revealed this truth: "Whoever believes in me will do the works I have been doing, and they will do even greater things."[5]

Jesus answered Peter's prayer, "Come," and Peter climbed out of the boat.[6] He walked on water! Peter's prayer was answered according to his expectation because of his faith. Faith is the invisible hand that reaches out and grasps the promises of God.

But then, Peter became afraid of the storm. Rational thought set in, and doubt creeped in along with it, and he started to drown. After Jesus pulled Peter up, He confirmed the reason for his drowning by saying, "O you of little faith, why did you doubt?"[7] Peter didn't start drowning because Jesus failed him. He started drowning because of his doubt.

Ask and Keep Believing

Peter's doubt is interesting, because he didn't start off with doubt. He started off full of faith. His doubt was evidence of a change in his beliefs.

To doubt is to waver in belief, and essentially to come out of agreement with God's Word. So the question is, Why did his belief change? How could someone who was already doing the impossible waver in his ability to continue? This is critical to understand because it gives us language for why we falter in our beliefs too.

First, understand that you're reading this book because you have the audacity to think that God can speak to you through dreams, that you can understand the language of your dreams, and that there's more available for you in growing in your intimacy with God. But *knowing* it's available and *believing* it's available *for you* are two different things. Believing it's available and keeping on believing are also two different things.

Peter, inspired by Jesus's moment of walking on water, prayed with faith to do the same. Jesus answered his prayer, and then Peter wavered. He went from looking at Jesus to looking at the storm, which is an illustration of self-reliance. He tried to reason his ability to continue amid the storm. But here's the funny part: The storm was there from the beginning. It only became an issue when his focus changed.

Perhaps you can relate to Peter. Have you ever prayed for something and while you were seeking God for it, you were fully dependent on God? Maybe you were praying, fasting, trusting— and then God gave it to you. But then your prayer life changed. You barely talked to God about it anymore. Your focus shifted from God to yourself.

There was a time when a friend of mine was in desperate need of a job. She prayed, fasted, and trusted God for favor—and she ended up getting a really good job! A couple of months later, she started experiencing a lot of frustration and was planning to quit. When she shared her plans with me, my first response was, "Have you prayed about it?" To my surprise, she hadn't. She realized she should be trusting the same God who provided her with a job beyond her expectations to also guide her with wisdom to navigate the tension at her workplace.

Fast-forward a couple of months, and the conflicts and frustrations were simply a few honest and humble conversations away from getting resolved. In her seeking God for wisdom and guidance, He spoke to her through dreams and showed her where she was in the wrong. She had taken offense and created a narrative about why people did what they did without ever speaking to them about the issues. At the time, her pride had blinded her from seeking truth.

I share this example because so often we pray and believe God for something, but then when He gives it to us, we stop believing in Him to help us sustain it.

It's common to have only enough faith for an initial experience, but it's important to recognize that building your faith requires effort and discipline. This is true for both natural and spiritual needs, and dreaming is no exception. God desires for you to not only encounter His voice but also regularly seek Him to gain clarity, direction, and insight for your life's path. This will only happen when your focus remains on God.

The good news is that you can learn to believe—and keep believing—that it's possible for you to receive and understand messages from God through your dreams. And the first step is to examine and uproot the hindrances to your faith.

Hindrances to Faith

Familiarity

Whenever I travel to a state or country for the first time, I'm excited to take in the location, try the top-rated restaurants, go sightseeing, and create a memorable experience. I become the kind of person who comes to California (where I live) and does the same thing, and I refer to it as "doing too much." The interesting part is that although we may judge the "tourist experience," it creates memories worth a lifetime, doing in just a few days things residents have never done, regardless of the number of years they've lived there. The reason is the assumption of familiarity.

Ironically, we are often ignorant of those things we assume we are most familiar with. Our assumptions don't match our lived experience.

During Jesus's time on the earth, after He was revealed as the Son of God, many began following Him and speaking of His authority and power and miraculous works. Then He visited His hometown. These were the people who knew Him as a baby. He grew up with their children. But their familiarity with Him was their greatest hindrance to experiencing the miraculous. Scripture tells us, "[Jesus] did not do many miracles there because of their lack of faith."[8] Their lack of faith was tied to their limited belief about the identity of Jesus. Regardless of the stories they had heard about Him, they couldn't see beyond what they already knew.

In our lives, we have a propensity to allow our past experiences with Christ to determine what's possible and available for our present and future. As a pastor, I often hear people say, "That's not how God speaks to me" when they hear about different ways to hear God's voice. You can never put the idea of what God "can" or "will" do in the little box of your experiences. The number of years you've lived is nothing compared to eternity, and we serve a God who exists outside of time. Eternity cannot contain Him, and your experiences barely scratch the surface of the possibilities with God.

If we are ever familiar with God, let us be familiar with the fact that we don't know the depths of His ability.

Ignorance

It's important to distinguish between healthy and unhealthy ignorance. Healthy ignorance is recognizing that there is much we don't yet know or understand about God and His ways. This humility can actually be a catalyst for deeper faith and trust in God. Unhealthy ignorance, on the other hand, is when we fail to seek the promises and possibilities God has already made available to us, including His communication with us through dreams. This lack of knowledge can lead to fear and uncertainty in our faith journey. This is why seeking knowledge and understanding of

God's Word is so important. It provides a foundation for our faith and allows us to anticipate what God will do in our lives with confidence and truth.

A great illustration is tandem skydiving, where one person is attached to an instructor who guides the entire jump—from exiting the plane in a free fall, to pulling the parachute, to landing safely on the ground. While I have always been intrigued by it, I'll admit, it's frightening, and though I've always wanted to try it, I haven't yet. When I watch videos of tandem skydiving, I notice an interesting contrast. The instructor is calm, often having a good time, smiling, and laughing. But the person attached to them often looks terrified. This begs the question—what's the difference? The answer is simple: knowledge.

Fear is often a result of what we don't know. Instructors are trained in proper procedures for every aspect of the jump, so even when faced with a potential threat or obstacle, they remain calm and are equipped to respond confidently. In the same way, when we seek knowledge and understanding of God's Word and His promises, we can face challenges with greater courage and trust, knowing that God is with us every step of the way, guiding us and equipping us for whatever may come. We become more confident and trusting in Him.

According to Isaiah 33:6, "Wisdom and knowledge will be the stability of your times." This is a powerful reminder that without knowledge and understanding of God's Word and promises, we can easily lose our footing and be shaken up by the challenges of life. But when we seek knowledge and grow in our understanding of God's Word, faith becomes the fruit of that understanding. This aligns with the message in Romans 10:17, which says that "faith comes by hearing, and hearing by the word of God."

When we immerse ourselves in God's Word and actively seek to understand its message, our faith is strengthened, giving us the stability and resilience we need to face life's challenges with calmness and confidence. When we encounter surprises or setbacks, our knowledge of God and His Word sustains us with the truth.

Disappointment

In November 2022, my aunt passed away from cancer. When we discovered she was sick, both immediate and extended family got together every day for a prayer call. We believed in God for supernatural healing. Nothing could shake our faith, so much so that even when she died, her eldest daughter, younger sister, and I went to the mortuary to not only see her body but to pray over it. My cousin started a video call with all her siblings, and we began to pray, believing that just as God raised Lazarus from the dead, He would also raise my aunt. I remember that morning, while we were getting ready to go to the mortuary, I was asked if I was nervous about seeing my aunt's dead body. I shared that I was more nervous about how to react when she *woke up.* I wasn't quite ready for the disappointment of ending our meeting at the mortuary picking out the casket for my aunt's funeral. She didn't get up. I had never seen faith on the level I experienced in myself and through my cousins, so as we left, I wondered, *All that for nothing?*

This is important to touch on because disappointment is like a cancer. If unchecked, it starts in one area and eventually spreads throughout your life. My story might not be yours, but if there's disappointment that hasn't been healed in your heart, then it's all the same. I didn't realize at the time how my aunt's death affected my prayer life. Subconsciously, I stopped seeking God with the same passion and hunger because I started believing that it didn't matter. At the end of the day, God would do what He desired. That was my mindset as a pastor, as a person who often shares her stories of encounters with God starting at nine years old. It was the mindset of someone who could testify to the miraculous power of faith and prayer. But this was also the person who believed wholeheartedly that God would heal her aunt—and He didn't.

> Hope is the heartbeat of our reliance and trust in God.

One day, while listening to some worship music, I broke down and cried out to the Lord. I wanted to know where He was. Why didn't He heal my aunt or raise her from the dead? Isn't that one of His promises? Then He reminded me about a truth regarding prayer, which is that prayer is not just demanding things from heaven. Prayer is also speaking what heaven demands. The Bible puts it this way: "Your will be done on earth as it is in heaven."[9]

The will of God triumphs over our will. He will never endorse something or answer that which is against His will and purpose. Even when we don't understand, He sees and makes decisions from an eternal perspective. This doesn't mean everything that happens is because of God's perfect will. Obviously, there's free will. But when we are watching for God to intervene in a matter, it's not simply about making our demands, but rather seeking to understand His will in each situation so we can agree with what He desires. Often this is realized by trial and error. It should never stop you from believing for the miraculous, but it should prompt you to seek God's plans and purpose even while you believe.

What I didn't mention is that before we even realized my aunt was sick, my older brother, who on certain occasions hears God's audible voice, shared with me that God told him it was my aunt's time to go home. When she became sick, despite what he had shared, I maintained hope and an expectation for her healing. While the outcome didn't align with my desire, hope is never wasted. Hope is the heartbeat of our reliance and trust in God, extending beyond our expectations to embrace His will.

Even Jesus had exceptions when it came to healing the people brought to Him. When He went to the pool of Bethesda,[10] a place with a great multitude of sick people, He healed only one man. It wasn't because the others lacked faith. Their presence at that location was evidence of their faith! Nevertheless, perhaps their healing wasn't aligned in the timing of God's will.

The reason I'm exploring the issue of disappointment is because of the impact it has on the heart. Proverbs 13:12 says, "Hope deferred makes the heart sick." If the heart is sick, wounded, or weak, it is challenging to truly believe God in other areas. No matter the disappointment you've faced, understand that God is for you. He desires for us to know His voice and deepen our intimacy with Him so that when disappointment comes, we'll remember that He is good and trustworthy. When it comes to knowing His voice, the hungry will never be disappointed.

Heavenly Father, thank You for the promise in Your Word, which declares, "Blessed are those who hunger and thirst for righteousness, for they shall be filled."[11] Thank You for healing the areas of my life that hindered my faith, restoring my hunger to believe once more. As a dreamer, I declare by faith that as I put into practice the teachings presented in this book, I will remember my dreams. When I present questions to You to understand the symbols within my dreams, I will have clarity and understanding of Your messages. In Jesus's name, amen.

Reflection Questions

1. Our behavior proves what we believe. What does your behavior say about your beliefs?

2. Which of the hindrances to faith feels most familiar to you? Why do you think that is?

NINE

THE DREAM-POWERED LIFE

It shall come to pass in the last days, says God,
That I will pour out of My Spirit on all flesh;
Your sons and your daughters shall prophesy,
Your young men shall see visions,
Your old men shall dream dreams.

—Acts 2:17

I have a dear friend who used to remember very little of her dreams. But a powerful encounter with God through a vision completely transformed her perspective on life and compelled her to turn to Him wholeheartedly. This pivotal experience led her to surrender her life to Jesus Christ, and as a result, she began to experience a remarkable increase in dream recall.

At first, many of these dreams seemed puzzling and had no apparent significance. But as we talked and prayed, seeking the guidance of the Holy Spirit, the veil lifted, and the true meaning behind the dreams became clear. It was through this process of interpretation that God's purpose and message were revealed, either resonating with a present situation in her life or serving as confirmation of future events.

As my friend began to recognize the importance of this form of communication with God, she decided to prioritize and create a lifestyle centered on hearing from Him. With this shift in her posture, she discovered that not only did her dreams increase in frequency, but their messages expanded beyond her immediate community. She became attuned to God's voice concerning not only herself and her family, close friends, and loved ones, but also in regards to her business and industry involvement. By faithfully stewarding the messages embedded within her dreams, she witnessed God entrusting her with insights and revelations that extended far beyond what she could have anticipated.

This newfound connectivity with God through her dreams opened up a realm of divine wisdom, discernment, and guidance. It allowed her to navigate personal challenges and make decisions with a heightened level of insight. Additionally, it positioned her as a vessel to impact others within her field, as God's wisdom flowed through her to bring transformation and divine alignment.

The Lord graciously bestowed upon her accurate prophetic insights regarding influential figures in her industry and the future developments within it. This divine communication granted her an advantage to conquer new territories and experience an elevation that was directly correlated to the revelations she received from God. Through her dreams, she perceived that her sphere of influence had expanded, for when God imparts revelation and insight, it signifies His support and empowerment in claiming new territories.

Remarkably, these assignments and opportunities had always been marked for her, but as He does with us, God in His wisdom revealed them to her as she diligently sought Him, making Him her utmost priority. It is important to note that she did not actively pursue influence; instead, she passionately maintained an attitude of never becoming complacent in the frequency of God's voice. As a result, her pursuit of deeper intimacy with Him caused His voice in her life to grow louder and clearer, unveiling profound truths that connected to her purpose and calling on earth.

God Seeks the Seeker

In the realm of heaven, a magnificent and awe-inspiring throne room exists, a place of absolute majesty and divine presence. At the heart of this chamber sits the Lord God Himself, adorned in regal splendor, radiating power and authority. Encircling this central throne are twenty-four smaller thrones, each occupied by esteemed elders adorned in glorious crowns crafted from the purest gold.

But the distinctiveness of the throne room extends beyond the presence of the twenty-four elders. Four extraordinary living creatures, unlike any ever witnessed on earth, are positioned near the central throne, their magnificent forms captivating all who behold them. These celestial beings are adorned with a multitude of eyes, an astonishing sight that attests to their unparalleled vision and perception. Each creature boasts six magnificent wings, imbued with divine attributes that set them apart from any earthly creature.

Intriguingly, these four living creatures are in a ceaseless state of worship and praise, their refrain echoing through the expanse. "Holy, holy, holy, Lord God Almighty, who was and is and is to come!"[1] they declare with fervor and devotion, their voices resounding throughout the throne room. Their chant serves as a perpetual reminder of the eternal nature of God's holiness and His unchanging existence, magnifying His unmatched power and glory.

Witnessing this profound scene, the twenty-four elders, positioned near the central throne, are moved by an overwhelming sense of reverence and adoration.[2] As an ultimate act of humility and worship, they prostrate themselves before the Lord God, casting their jeweled crowns at His feet. In this act, they acknowledge the incomparable worthiness of the Lord, recognizing His unique position as the Creator of all things. With sincere hearts, the elders proclaim, "You are worthy, O Lord, to receive glory and honor and power; for You created all things, and by Your will they exist and were created."[3] Their words encapsulate the profound truth that all things owe their existence to the divine will of the Creator.

Try to envision the divine scene before you. Picture God seated upon His majestic throne, radiating with awe-inspiring glory. In the midst of this captivating image, four creatures stand out, each adorned with their own unique features. But what truly captures your attention is their extraordinary display of eyes, encompassing their entire beings. This detail holds great significance, for their constant declaration of "holy, holy, holy" is not a mere religious ritual. No, it is a genuine expression of wonder and awe, as if each time they lay their eyes upon God, a new revelation of His eternal nature is unveiled. They reverentially acknowledge Him as the one "who was and is and is to come!" This unceasing worship within the throne room is the result of an everlasting encounter with the ever-unfolding dimensions and insights found in beholding the Lord God.

This vivid depiction serves as a reminder that there is an infinite depth to God that must not be overlooked. We cannot afford to become complacent with the mundanity of our daily experiences, seeking after Him only in times of crisis or need. Such a limited perspective diminishes our true potential and robs us of the rich calling upon our lives. Instead, let us adopt the mindset of these beings, who continually explore and uncover the unfathomable depths of God's glory. Let us approach each day with a hunger to encounter new facets of His character, to uncover fresh revelations of His love and power. In doing so, we will live a life that transcends the ordinary. For there is an inexhaustible wellspring of treasures waiting to be discovered in God, and it is our privilege and joy to embark on the journey of exploration and revelation.

In our relentless pursuit of God, He graciously unveils deeper truths about ourselves that would otherwise remain hidden. These truths are reserved for those earnestly seeking Him, eager to know Him more intimately. An illuminating scripture that highlights this concept is Proverbs 25:2, which poignantly states, "It is the glory of God to conceal a matter, but the glory of kings is to search out a matter."

Just as a man's pursuit of a woman reveals his true intentions and perception of her worth, our pursuit of God speaks volumes about our understanding of His value and significance in our lives. If a man's pursuit of a romantic interest shows that he is unwilling to selflessly prioritize and cherish what is important to her, it serves as a warning sign that any true friend would bring to her attention. Pursuit, in this context, goes beyond mere outward actions of chasing after something or someone. It is a posture of devoted desire toward a person or cause.

Marriage serves as an example of the importance of unceasing pursuit. Even after we enter the covenant of marriage, wisdom dictates that we should never cease pursuing our spouse. It extends beyond accomplishing a specific goal; it is a perpetual posture of devotion. Similarly, in our relationship with God, we must recognize that our perception of His worth is intimately connected to our constant pursuit of Him.

> Existing without purposeful direction is not true living; it is mere existence.

If we gauge the value of our natural relationships based on our pursuit of them, how much more should we prioritize and pursue an authentic and deep relationship with God? Let us embrace the truth that in our unwavering quest for God, not only do we discover more of Him, but He also reveals profound truths about us.

God's inclination to hide things is not meant to keep them concealed, but it does ignite a hunger within us. In our pursuit, we are granted revelation, insights, and profound mysteries that empower us to walk in the fullness of our God-ordained purpose, predetermined even before we existed.[4]

The ultimate pursuit in life, the one that truly matters, is the quest for intimacy with God. He alone is the source of our very existence. When God created the fish and creatures in the sea, God commanded the waters to bring them forth.[5] Yet when God created humanity, He spoke to Himself, saying, "Let Us make man in Our image, according to Our likeness."[6] He is our origin.

Just as a fish perishes when removed from its life-giving source, without being rooted in God, we wither away. Though our hearts still beat and blood courses through our veins, we are severed from the wellspring of true life. Existing without purposeful direction is not true living; it is mere existence. Hence, Jesus declared, "I am the vine, you are the branches. He who abides in Me, and I in him, bears much fruit; for without Me you can do nothing."[7]

While I have explored in various ways throughout this book how seeking God positions us to hear from Him, in this final chapter, I want to delve into the manner in which we seek Him, and how a mature pursuit can expand our capacity for receiving dreams from God on a daily basis.

Spiritual Maturity

The journey of motherhood has led me to a deeper understanding of my own mother and the decisions she made during my childhood. Parenting my daughter has provided me with a new perspective on the complexities of motherhood. As a child, it is common to encounter restrictions that seem unwarranted. This often stems from the divergent viewpoints between the child and the parent(s). From the child's perspective, they believe they know what is best for them, while a wise and loving parent recognizes the need to set boundaries and regulate certain aspects of their child's life due to their limited knowledge and understanding of the world.

Maturity serves as evidence of a renewed mind and an evolved way of thinking, living, and being. The apostle Paul eloquently expressed this concept, stating, "When I was a child, I spoke and thought and reasoned as a child. But when I grew up, I put away childish things."[8] As we mature, our perspectives shift, and we gain a deeper understanding of the reasoning behind previous restrictions. This growth allows us to appreciate our parents' love, wisdom, and desire to protect and guide us throughout our childhood.

In our relationship with God, He meets us where we are but doesn't intend for us to stay stagnant. It is easy to mistake God's provision, communication, and intimacy in the place where He initially meets us as a sign that further growth is unnecessary. We become comfortable with our routines and patterns because they have proven effective for us, without realizing that there is a greater depth of connection with God available to us as we spiritually mature.

I have vivid memories of receiving dreams from God since I was nine years old. Throughout my journey, I have experienced various highs and lows in my walk with Him. Even during times of rebellion, I still heard God's voice, though the depth and complexity of His messages were tailored to match my level of spiritual maturity at the time.

Maturity in our faith journey with Christ is not a passive process, but rather an active decision to die to ourselves. It requires a daily commitment to surrender our own will and desires in order to align with God's will for our lives. The apostle John, who wrote the book of Revelation, serves as a powerful example of this kind of commitment. He was exiled to the island of Patmos because of his dedication to God's assignment.[9] It's no coincidence that Patmos means "my killing" and that in this place of isolation and apparent death John was given access to profound revelations about Jesus Christ and the events of the end times.[10]

One of those revelations was the powerful scene in the throne room that I referenced at the beginning of this chapter.

Dying to self is not a supernatural gift bestowed upon us; rather, it is a conscious decision we make to pursue more of God. Jesus Himself exemplified this in His statement, "I lay down My life."[11] He actively and intentionally chose to surrender His life for the benefit of others. The beauty of recognizing that dying to self is within our power is that it can be cultivated and practiced. There are specific actions and disciplines that we can engage in to foster the pursuit of God's will above our own selfish ambitions. Throughout this book, we have explored various disciplines. In this chapter, we will examine three key areas that should become a lifestyle for believers seeking to deepen their relationship with God: prayer, fasting, and meditation. These three practices are not meant to be isolated, occasional practices, but rather integral components of a mature and vibrant faith. They should become woven into the fabric of our lives, creating space for God to shape us as we deepen our relationship with Him. The dream-powered life is a life surrendered to God. As we commit to a lifestyle of actively pursuing God through these disciplines, the maturity in our pursuit of Him will set the stage for His Word to be made known through our lives.

Prayer

I have learned to view prayer in three distinct ways: asking, seeking, and knocking. Jesus, in His teachings on prayer, mentioned these levels: "Ask, and it will be given to you; seek, and you will find; knock, and it will be opened to you."[12] This particular scripture has profoundly shaped my perspective on how we approach

God through prayer. It emphasizes that our prayer life should be characterized by intentionality, passion, and persistence. It teaches us that there are hidden treasures and blessings available to us, waiting to be discovered as we posture ourselves and diligently pursue God.

When we engage in the first level of prayer, asking, we are posturing ourselves to inquire of God. By asking, we are acknowledging our dependence on God and His ability to provide for our spiritual and natural needs.

Moving to the second level, seeking, indicates our earnest desire to comprehend and align our requests with God's will and His Word for our lives. This level of prayer enables us to access His thoughts, plans, and purposes for us. As we seek after God's will, we open ourselves up to receiving divine guidance and direction.

The third level, knocking, represents a deeper level of seeking. When we knock, we are actively seeking entrance into a place that we believe is within the will of God for us. But this level often presents obstacles and resistance. The door may not readily open, and we may face challenges and setbacks. Nevertheless, through persistent knocking, with an expectation that the door is meant to be opened to us, we can ultimately access the blessings and opportunities that lie on the other side.

These three levels of prayer—asking, seeking, and knocking—serve as a road map for our approach to God. They encourage us to engage in meaningful and intentional conversation with Him, seeking His wisdom, guidance, and provision. By embracing the principles embodied in these levels, we can deepen our relationship with God and experience the abundant life that He desires for us.

So how do we practically apply these truths to our prayer life? How can we navigate the barriers that stand between where we are and where God is calling us to be? One key insight into this mystery is the practice of praying in the Spirit.

Praying in the Spirit, often misunderstood as a mystical or exclusive practice, is akin to speaking in our original native language. Just as people from different countries have their own unique languages, our true place of origin is not on earth but in God. When we pray in the Spirit, we are connecting with our original native language. (Remember, you started with God.)

Praying in the Spirit, also known as praying in tongues, is a way of communication enabled by the Holy Spirit. It may seem unfamiliar or strange to some, but it is a powerful means of tapping into the depths of God's will. Through this practice, we can communicate in a language that transcends human understanding and connects directly with God. When we pray in the Spirit, we engage in a form of prayer that surpasses our own limited understanding and touches the heart of God. It is a means by which we align ourselves with His will.

Praying in the Spirit can be likened to knocking on the right door, as it's not just about the act itself but also about the person behind the door. The difference between being seen as an intruder or being an invited and expected guest lies in whose door we are knocking on. Sometimes we may feel like we're knocking on doors that are not opening for us. These doors may serve our selfish ambitions and be rooted in wrong motives. But these are not the doors that God intends to open for us. James 4:3 explains that when we ask with wrong motives, we do not receive, as our desires are focused on self-indulgence.

When we pray in the Spirit, we align ourselves with the perfect will of God.[13] The Spirit of God prays through us, expressing the mind of God for our lives. In this form of prayer, our own mind and will are not involved, leaving no room for selfish ambition to interfere. Instead, we are able to speak in alignment and agreement with God's desires.

When we communicate with God in this manner, we are speaking mysteries in the Spirit.[14] We utter things that we haven't even come to know or understand through natural knowledge. Just imagine God's response to such dialogue. It opens up a deeper level of conversation, revelation, and insight that surpasses our natural comprehension.

When we pray in the Spirit, our conversation with God can continue through channels of communication like dreams. I have noticed that when I spend time praying in the Spirit, whether it's for a few minutes or an hour during my day, or especially before going to bed, I often have encounters with the Lord or deeply insightful and prophetic dreams about future events.

Many people hesitate to pray in the Spirit because they find it strange or worry that it may sound like gibberish. But God uses prayer to bring us closer to Him, revealing our reliance on the Lord. It's not meant to be a picture-perfect activity; after all, you are speaking to your Creator, not a romantic interest. When you make a habit of praying in the Spirit, even if it starts with just a few minutes each day, you cultivate a posture of dependency on God and acknowledge your limitations in knowledge. In addition to praying in the languages you speak about the things you already know, you can also pray in your heavenly language to tap into the mysteries connected to your life. And as you persist in prayer, be watchful in your dreams for God's messages.

I would be misguided to assume that every reader is familiar with the concept of praying in the Spirit. There is a common misunderstanding that praying in the Spirit is a definitive proof of receiving the Holy Spirit. This misconception often leads to shame and doubt, causing individuals to question if they truly have given their lives to Jesus. But this belief is a misinterpretation of the Scriptures, specifically the account in Acts 2 where the Holy Spirit descended upon the twelve apostles and enabled them to speak in tongues.

The tongues spoken by the apostles in Acts 2 were manifestations of the ability to speak in different languages, including both earthly languages and spiritual tongues.[15] In this instance, the tongues spoken were of different earthly languages that could be understood by the diverse group of people present at that time.[16] This event was not primarily about prayer to God, but rather about the apostles serving as vessels through which the Holy Spirit ministered to reach people from various parts of the world.

The phenomenon that occurred on that day was supernatural, as the apostles were not originally proficient in these languages. It was the power of the Holy Spirit, who possesses knowledge of all earthly languages, that enabled them to glorify God in this way. It is important to note that speaking in tongues is not the definitive mark of receiving the Holy Spirit.

The true indication of having received the Holy Spirit is the inner conviction that you are a child of God after accepting Jesus as your Savior.[17] Praying in the Spirit is one of the manifestations of the Holy Spirit, along with others like prophecy or working of miracles.[18] These manifestations are activated by a genuine desire driven by the right motives.[19] Many people haven't tapped into this because they lack understanding of its significance and, as a result, don't truly desire it.

God doesn't want to withhold the ability to pray in the Spirit from you. Why would He want to limit your ability to pray according to His perfect will for your life? He is for you, and if you desire to pray in the Spirit, and are willing to let the Spirit pray through you, it will come.

Here's an additional tip: If you desire to pray in the Spirit but haven't been consistent in daily prayer in your earthly language(s), start there. As you continue to seek God and expect Him to release the manifestation of praying in the Spirit in your life, be patient and remain open and available to the leading of the Holy Spirit.

Fasting

Every believer should live a life marked by prayer and fasting, as this was the lifestyle exemplified by Jesus Himself. He has called us to live on earth as He did, empowered by the Holy Spirit.[20] Fasting is a practice that draws us deeper into intimacy and partnership with God, allowing Him to shape and guide our lives according to His perfect plan. Through fasting and seeking Him wholeheartedly, we become more sensitive to His voice and communication, including through our dreams.

Fasting is not about getting what we want, but about aligning our hearts with God's will and drawing closer to Him. It is a way to consecrate and make ourselves more available to hear from Him.

Fasting is a form of worship where we fix our attention on the Lord, making Him the object of our affection. It is not simply about denying our physical appetites, but rather about embracing the desires of the Spirit. When we view fasting as an act of worship, it becomes a regular part of our lifestyle, not just a response to challenges we face. While there are biblical examples of seeking God through fasting in difficult times, when we approach fasting as worship, it takes us into a deeper level of intimacy with God.

When we engage in fasting as an act of proactive intimacy, we establish a rhythm that is unique to our individual lives. This could involve fasting once a week, setting aside three days each month, or establishing a specific cadence that suits you.

Through fasting, we humble our souls. As King David expressed in Psalm 35:13, fasting is a way of humbling ourselves. Our soul encompasses our wisdom and intellect, and when we fast, we willingly lay it all down. We separate ourselves from the busyness and distractions that constantly surround us in order to spend more time in God's presence and the study of His Word. In this place of humility, we allow ourselves to receive His wisdom, revelation, and guidance to direct our lives.

Fasting extends beyond simply abstaining from food. While food was the focus during biblical times, it is important to note that they did not have the multitude of distractions that we have today, such as social media and streaming apps. Back then, cooking was a process, requiring time and effort. By abstaining from food, they were able to dedicate more time to seeking after God.

Scripture has many examples of how fasting opens us up to receive God's word. In Acts 13:2, as Paul and Barnabas were seeking the Lord through fasting, the Holy Spirit spoke to them about their calling. When fasting becomes a lifestyle, it consistently positions us to have a hunger for God's word. This hunger is not an anointing but is a result of not being filled with distractions. We are able to enter into a deeper level of communion and conversation with Him. As a result, we can expect to experience vivid and frequent dreams.

Meditation

The concept of meditation is often associated with cultural practices that focus on emptying the mind, controlling breathing, and achieving a heightened sense of self-consciousness. But when we approach meditation from a biblical perspective, we gain a deeper awareness of the presence, will, and attributes of God in our thoughts.

Biblical meditation does not aim to empty the mind but rather to fill it with God's Word so that it may take root and transform our way of thinking. It deepens our understanding of God and leads us to a greater sense of awe in His presence.

This type of meditation involves a reflective and intentional focus on God's Word and His character. It goes beyond simply reading the Scriptures and delves into pondering, contemplating, and internalizing them. By doing so, we gain understanding, wisdom, and spiritual insight. As we dwell on God's Word, it shapes our hearts and minds and guides our actions. Through this practice, we deepen our connection with God and cultivate a profound reverence for His presence in our lives.

The Bible consistently emphasizes the significance and positive impact of meditation. Isaiah 26:3 teaches us that through the practice of meditation, we can cultivate a deep trust in God, leading to the remarkable outcome of dwelling in perfect peace. Psalm 1:2 portrays the blessed individual as someone who takes delight in the law of the Lord and engages in continual meditation upon it.

Through meditation, we actively connect with God's Word, His character, and His ways. We engage in practices such as reading, repeating, and reflecting on Scripture. As we meditate on these truths, they transition from being mere information to becoming personal revelations of who God truly is. In this process, meditation becomes an avenue for deepening our understanding and intimate knowledge of our Creator.

> Biblical meditation does not aim to empty the mind but rather to fill it with God's Word.

As I reflect on a specific morning during my prayer time, I vividly remember bringing my anxieties about childbirth before God. In that moment, the truth of God's omnipresence came to mind. I began to contemplate what it truly means for God to be present everywhere at the same time. In that stillness, a scripture surfaced in my thoughts: "the Alpha and the Omega," symbolizing God as the beginning and end of all things.[21] It struck me that God's presence transcends the constraints of time.

An insight dawned on me: God isn't simply in every place in the present moment, but He also resides within everything, encompassing the past, the present, and the future. This realization led me to a profound understanding that I can trust Him with my tomorrow because He is already there. He is already present in the labor room. And the same is true for you. Whatever challenge or difficulty you're facing, God is already present there. Whatever conversation you're dreading or task you're avoiding, He is already there. This revelation dispelled my fears, filling me with a deep sense of peace and hope for the future. What began as anxious thoughts transformed into a worshipful awe of God, my recognition that there is truly none like Him. This experience deepened my reverence for our almighty God.

Psalm 25:14 imparts a profound truth: "The secret of the Lord is with those who fear Him, and He will show them His covenant." The importance of meditation in the life of every believer lies in its ability to cultivate a reverential fear of the Lord. This isn't a fear that torments or cripples, but rather an awe and deep reverence for God.

Many individuals simply read the Bible to gain knowledge about God, yet their lives remain unaffected. There is no visible transformation, and when storms arise, they question God's presence and support. But through the practice of meditation, our understanding of God deepens, shaping our perspective and drawing us closer to Him. In this process, God begins to reveal intimate secrets and truths to us. Our communion with God deepens as we engage with the various ways He speaks to us, including through our dreams.

Before going to bed, I often engage in meditation focused on a specific attribute of God. During some of those nights, in my dreams, I have encountered Him and received teachings. It is important to remember that our time on earth is limited, and we should not wait until we reach heaven to pursue a deeper relationship with God. Our journey into His depths begins here on earth.

Through our dreams, we have the opportunity to experience encounters that reveal the hidden things of God. But this hinges on our posture and lifestyle. If we adopt the identity of a seeker, constantly pursuing God, He will draw us deeper into Himself.

I often find it fitting to compare our spiritual journey to the vastness of the galaxy, with its countless stars and planets stretching across unimaginable distances. The complexity of the galaxy remains a mystery to astronomers, as they constantly uncover new facets while acknowledging that there is still so much more to comprehend. Yet the grandeur of the galaxy is merely a small fragment of the immense knowledge of God. His wisdom extends far beyond the boundaries of the galaxy, encompassing all of creation and existence. In our ongoing relationship with Him, there are always greater depths to explore and discover. Even eternity itself would not provide enough time to fully fathom the vastness of His divine being. It is for this reason that we must adopt the mindset and lifestyle of a seeker, forever yearning to explore the mysteries of God.

The Night Is the Beginning

There is an intriguing detail in the story of creation: The Bible presents evening as the beginning of the day. Genesis 1:5 enlightens us with the statement, "the evening and the morning were the first day." Here, evening refers to nighttime. Although we traditionally perceive a new day to commence when we wake up in the morning, there is beauty in recognizing that our day truly begins in the early hours of the night.

When we grasp the understanding that our dreams serve as a conduit for divine revelation and insight from God, we gain a fresh perspective on how these nocturnal visions empower us for the coming day. Dreams possess the remarkable ability to provide us with wisdom, guidance, and understanding that can shape our thoughts, decisions, and actions. They offer a unique encounter with the spiritual realm, where communication with God takes place within the depths of our subconscious mind.

By fully embracing the importance of dreams, we come to realize that our relationship with God extends beyond the confines of our waking hours. We understand that the revelations we receive through our dreams provide us with spiritual discernment that profoundly influences our interactions, choices, and reactions in the world. This recognition of the value of dreams empowers us to live a life fueled by their divine guidance, infusing each new day with renewed purpose and a heightened sense of clarity.

Heavenly Father, thank You for encountering me in my sleep. I have been equipped with truth to live a dream-empowered life. As I embrace a lifestyle of prayer, fasting, and meditation, I will experience a renewed closeness with You, deepening my intimacy in communion with You. This transformative journey will leave me forever changed. In Jesus's name, amen.

Reflection Questions

1. How do you seek God currently? How would you like to seek God?

2. What does a dream-empowered life mean to you?

THE DREAMER'S JOURNEY

The ability to experience God-given dreams serves as a testament to His profound love for us. It has always been God's desire, from the very beginning of creation, to be the guiding voice in our lives and lead us toward a purposeful and impactful existence. He knows us intimately, for we are created in His image. From the beginning, He chose to be present with humanity in the garden, accessible at all times without any barrier to communion. Unfortunately, sin introduced a barrier between humanity and God. Yet the purity of God's love that inspired our creation remained unaltered.

Jesus, despite His divine nature, humbled Himself and took on the form of humanity, being born into His own creation. He did this with the purpose of offering His life as a living sacrifice for all of humankind, regardless of whether they embrace or accept Him. The sacrifice of Jesus on the cross holds immense significance in our journey toward intimacy with God. Through His selfless act, Jesus bore the weight of humanity's sin, acting as the bridge that reconciled us with the Father. His sacrifice cleared the path for us to have direct access to the boundless love and presence of God, removing all barriers and limitations.

By paying the price for sin, Jesus not only revealed the depth of His love for us but also made it possible for us to experience genuine intimacy with God. Jesus's sacrifice was not in vain, as it was intended to restore a close and personal relationship with each of us.

He didn't die for us to later not speak to us.

Through His death and resurrection, Jesus demolished the barrier that separated us from God, obliterating the need for intermediaries or sacrifices to connect with Him. His selfless act brought forth restoration and redemption, granting us the privilege to approach the throne of grace with boldness and confidence. Jesus's sacrifice on the cross restored the open invitation to intimately know and commune with God, akin to the close relationship Adam and Eve shared in the garden. As a result, our dreams transcend mere random images or fragments of imagination. They become a conduit for divine revelation and guidance. Our dreams transform into a blank canvas where God can paint His visions and insights, illuminating our path as we journey through life. In the depths of our subconscious, God plants the seeds of His plans and purposes, bringing forth clarity, direction, and a profound sense of purpose. During the silent hours of the night, through our dreams, God communicates His heart to ours. Our dreams turn into a sacred space of encounter, leading us into the depths of His heart, unveiling His plans for our lives.

But the journey of the dreamer does not conclude with the ability to consistently receive God-given dreams. It is merely the beginning. Our communion with God is not limited to the hours we sleep and dream, for there are numerous opportunities for intimacy with Him throughout our waking hours as well. In chapter 1, we explored different ways in which we can experience the voice of God—by feeling, knowing, hearing, and seeing. All these realms are available to you, and as you have exercised faith in tapping into the power of your dreams, do not stop there.

Your journey is ultimately one of deepening intimacy with God, which can be strengthened with dreams. Embrace the fullness of what it means to intimately know and commune with Him, both in your dreams and in your waking moments. God has much to show you.

ACKNOWLEDGMENTS

"Two are better than one, because they have a good reward for their labor."[1] The collective efforts and contributions of many have made the completion of this book a significant reward.

I am most grateful to almighty God for the privilege to steward this revelation. Dreams have consistently been a landscape for Your voice to me, and now You have entrusted me with the assignment to awaken this generation to the power of their dreams.

To my husband, Ifeanyi Okafor, thank you for being my rock, covering, supporter, and encourager. I appreciate the space you created for me to write and the inspiring conversations that shaped the context of this book.

To my mother, Esther Ike, your support in helping care for Ariel during her first three months while I finished the book goes beyond words. Thank you, Mum, for always pushing me to be better and grounding me with the belief that I can achieve anything I set my mind to.

To my pastor and spiritual father, Touré Roberts, thank you for your continued leadership, love, and guidance.

To my literary agent, Andrea Heinecke, thank you for that introductory email that led to this journey. I am grateful to you and everyone at The Bindery.

To my editor, Estee Zandee, your patience and steadfastness have been invaluable. Your exceptional feedback has significantly shaped this book. You are a true gem. Thank you!

To the entire team at WaterBrook and Multnomah, thank you for embarking on this journey with me and believing in the vision of this book.

To Amanda McIntire of the Mac Creative Agency, your brilliance in the creative direction for the book cover is deeply appreciated.

To Brian and Kim Freeman, thank you for flawlessly capturing the photography for the book cover.

To everyone mentioned in this book, thank you for the shared experiences and the impact these stories will have on a generation awakening to the power of their dreams.

NOTES

Introduction

1. Exodus 33:11.
2. Bible Study, s.v. "Horeb," BibleStudy.org, accessed January 5, 2024, www.biblestudy.org/meaning-names/sinai-horeb.html.
3. Genesis 2:21–22.
4. Jay Summer, "8 Health Benefits of Sleep," Sleep Foundation, June 27, 2023, www.sleepfoundation.org/how-sleep-works/benefits-of-sleep.
5. Gemma Curtis, "Your Life in Numbers," Sleep Matters Club, March 31, 2023, www.dreams.co.uk/sleep-matters-club/your-life-in-numbers-infographic.

Chapter One: God Speaks to You

1. A. W. Tozer, *The Pursuit of God: Updated Edition with Study Guide* (Edinburgh: Waymark, 2020).
2. Romans 1:20; Colossians 1:16.
3. John 16:13.
4. Exodus 4:14.
5. Exodus 33:19.
6. Proverbs 6:16.
7. Psalm 104:31.
8. Mark 10:17.
9. Mark 10:21, NASB.
10. Mark 10:22, NASB.
11. Isaiah 9:6.
12. Romans 5:8.
13. Romans 8:31.

14. Romans 8:28.
15. 1 Corinthians 12:9.
16. Matthew 4:19.
17. 1 Samuel 3:20.
18. We see prophets leading regions and groups of people and giving counsel to leaders throughout the Bible, such as Moses in Exodus 19, Elijah in 1 Kings 18, "the man of God" in 1 Kings 13, Huldah in 2 Chronicles 34:14–33, and Deborah in Judges 4:4–5, among others.
19. 1 Corinthians 14:1–3.
20. 1 Corinthians 14:3.
21. 1 Samuel 3:3–11.
22. 1 Samuel 10:6.
23. Matthew 10:19–20.
24. "Why Good Vision Is So Important," Zeiss, October 16, 2021, www.zeiss.com/vision-care/us/better-vision/health-prevention/why-good-vision-is-so-important.html.
25. Strong's Greek Lexicon, s.v. "apokalypsis," Blue Letter Bible, www.blueletterbible.org/lexicon/g602/kjv/tr/0-1.
26. Revelation 1:11.
27. 2 Kings 6:17.
28. 1 Samuel 3:1.

Chapter Two: You the Dreamer

1. Matthew 6:11.
2. John 4:34.
3. "Brain Basics: Understanding Sleep," National Institute of Neurological Disorders and Stroke, accessed January 6, 2024, www.ninds.nih.gov/health-information/public-education/brain-basics/brain-basics-understanding-sleep.
4. Helder Bértolo et al., "Rapid Eye Movements (REMs) and Visual Dream Recall in Both Congenitally Blind and Sighted Subjects," Proceedings of SPIE 10453 (August 22, 2017): 104532C, https://doi.org/10.1117/12.2276048.
5. Eric Suni and Alex Dimitriu, "Dreams," Sleep Foundation, last modified December 8, 2023, www.sleepfoundation.org/articles/dreams-and-sleep.
6. "What Does It Mean When We Dream?" Medical News Today, last modified April 22, 2022, www.medicalnewstoday.com/articles/284378.
7. Matthew 2:2.

8. Matthew 2:13–14.
9. Jeff Jacoby, "The Undeferred Dreams of Elias Howe and Madame C. J. Walker," *Boston Globe,* March 23, 2018, www.bostonglobe.com/opinion/2018/03/23/the-undeferred-dreams-elias-howe-and-madame-walker/GA3ajqwnq4UiVoFe3HQERP/story.html.
10. Mark Cannizzario, Brett Cyrgalis, and George Willis, "Top 10 Golfers of All Time: The Post's Experts Make Their Cases," *New York Post,* May 14, 2019, https://nypost.com/2019/05/14/top-10-golfers-of-all-time-the-posts-experts-makes-their-cases.
11. Lisa D. Mickey, "Golf the Way You Dreamed It Would Be," *New York Times,* July 1, 2012, https://archive.nytimes.com/onpar.blogs.nytimes.com/2012/07/01/golf-the-way-you-dreamed-it-would-be.
12. Erick Massoto, "James Cameron Reveals 'Avatar' Franchise Came to Him in a Dream," Collider, November 24, 2022, https://collider.com/avatar-origin-story-james-cameron-dream-comments.
13. Matthew 27:18.
14. Matthew 27:19.
15. Matthew 27:24.
16. Mark 6:52.
17. Strong's Greek Lexicon, s.v. "pōroō," Blue Letter Bible, www.blueletterbible.org/lexicon/g4456/kjv/tr/0-1.
18. Matthew 27:3–5.
19. John 12:6.
20. Matthew 26:15.
21. John 13:27.
22. 1 John 4:8.
23. Tim Thornborough, "5 Ideas to Turn the Conversation to Jesus on Halloween," The Good Book Company, October 25, 2018, www.thegoodbook.com/blog/interestingthoughts/2018/10/25/5-ideas-to-turn-the-conversation-to-jesus-on-hallo.
24. Marianne Williamson, "Our Deepest Fear," Appleseeds.org, accessed January 7, 2024, www.appleseeds.org/Deepest-Fear.htm.
25. John 1:1.

Chapter Three: Prepare Your Body and Soul

1. 2 Kings 4:2.
2. Genesis 2:7.
3. Watchman Nee, *The Spiritual Man* (New York: Christian Fellowship Publishers, Inc., 1968), 27.

4. Psalm 143:3.
5. 2 Timothy 1:7.
6. "The BURGER KING® Brand Creates a Halloween Sandwich Clinically Proven to Induce Nightmares," Business Wire, October 17, 2018, www.businesswire.com/news/home/20181017005208/en/BURGER-KING®-Brand-Creates-Halloween-Sandwich-Clinically-Proven-to-Induce-Nightmares.
7. Elise Mandl, "The 7 Worst Foods for Your Brain," Healthline, updated March 14, 2023, www.healthline.com/nutrition/worst-foods-for-your-brain.
8. Rachel Welch, "The Reciprocal Relationship Between Nutrition and Dreams," Health by Principle, September 23, 2022, www.healthby principle.com/blogs/news/the-reciprocal-relationship-between-nutrition-and-dreams.
9. Genesis 2:2–3.
10. 1 Kings 19:12.
11. Galatians 5:22–23.
12. Hebrews 12:11, NIV.

Chapter Four: The Source of Dreams

1. Jeremiah 29:11.
2. Deuteronomy 6:4.
3. Matthew 4:4.
4. Matthew 4:6.
5. Matthew 4:7.
6. Genesis 22:2.
7. Hebrews 11:19.
8. Galatians 5:22–23.
9. Revelation 12:7–9.
10. John 16:13.
11. John 8:44, NIV.
12. Luke 4:2.
13. Luke 4:3.
14. John 5:19, NIV.
15. Luke 4:13.
16. Psalm 118:17.
17. 2 Corinthians 10:5, NIV.

18. Galatians 5:17, 19–21.
19. 1 Corinthians 15:31.
20. Jeremiah 29:8.

Chapter Five: Types of Dreams

1. Matthew 13:10.
2. Matthew 13:11.
3. Matthew 13:18–23.
4. Psalm 119:105, NLT.
5. Isaiah 6:8.
6. 1 Thessalonians 5:5, ESV.
7. Genesis 12:1.
8. Acts 16:6–10.
9. Genesis 31:10–13.
10. 1 Kings 3:5, NLT.
11. 1 Corinthians 12:7–10.
12. Jeremiah 29:13.
13. 1 Peter 5:5–6.
14. Romans 8:28.
15. Deuteronomy 34:9.
16. Proverbs 3:6, ESV.
17. Psalm 23:1.
18. Proverbs 10:22.
19. Jeff Jacoby, "The Undeferred Dreams of Elias Howe and Madame C. J. Walker," *Boston Globe,* March 23, 2018, www.bostonglobe.com /opinion/2018/03/23/the-undeferred-dreams-elias-howe-and-madame-walker/GA3ajqwnq4UiVoFe3HQERP/story.html.
20. A'Lelia Bundles, *On Her Own Ground: The Life and Times of Madam C. J. Walker* (New York: Scribner, 2002).
21. Genesis 41.
22. Psalm 34:4.
23. Genesis 28:18.
24. Proverbs 14:12.
25. "President Lincoln Dreams About His Assassination," History.com, April 1, 2020, www.history.com/this-day-in-history/lincoln-dreams-about-a-presidential-assassination.
26. Genesis 20:3–7.

27. Genesis 2:24.
28. 1 Corinthians 6:17.
29. Ezekiel 6:9.
30. Revelation 22:15.
31. Psalm 23:6.
32. Isaiah 21:6.
33. Strong's Hebrew Lexicon, s.v. "ṣāp̄â," Blue Letter Bible, www
   .blueletterbible.org/lexicon/h6822/kjv/wlc/0-1.
34. Ezekiel 33:7.
35. Luke 22:32.
36. 1 Kings 18:1.
37. James 5:17–18.
38. Psalm 115:16.
39. Luke 2:36–38.
40. Matthew 6:9–13.

Chapter Six: The Interpretation of Dreams

1. Genesis 40:8.
2. Genesis 1:28.
3. John 14:12.
4. Genesis 40:9–13, NLT.
5. Hebrews 6:1.
6. Ephesians 6:12, NIV.
7. Isaiah 8:19.
8. Matthew 17:2.
9. Matthew 7:15.
10. 2 Corinthians 12:9.
11. John 14:15–17.
12. Luke 1:19, NIV.

Chapter Seven: The Power of God's Word

1. Jeremiah 1:5.
2. 1 Kings 17:9.
3. Strong's Hebrew Lexicon, Blue Letter Bible, s.v. "ṣāvâ," www

.blueletterbible.org/lexicon/h6680/esv/wlc/0-1, and "nāṯan," www
.blueletterbible.org/lexicon/h5414/kjv/wlc/0-1.

4. Jeremiah 1:5.
5. Genesis 1:1–3.
6. Strong's Hebrew Lexicon, s.v. "hāyâ," Blue Letter Bible, www
   .blueletterbible.org/lexicon/h1961/kjv/wlc/0-1.
7. John 1:3.
8. A'Lelia Bundles, *On Her Own Ground: The Life and Times of Madam
   C. J. Walker* (New York: Scribner, 2002).
9. Bundles, *On Her Own Ground.*

Chapter Eight: Access through Faith

1. Mark 5:34.
2. James 5:15.
3. Matthew 14:26.
4. Matthew 14:28.
5. John 14:12, NIV.
6. Matthew 14:29.
7. Matthew 14:31.
8. Matthew 13:58, NIV.
9. Matthew 6:10.
10. John 5.
11. Matthew 5:6.

Chapter Nine: The Dream-Powered Life

1. Revelation 4:8.
2. Revelation 4:10.
3. Revelation 4:11.
4. Jeremiah 1:5.
5. Genesis 1:20.
6. Genesis 1:26.
7. John 15:5.
8. 1 Corinthians 13:11, NLT.
9. Revelation 1:9.

10. Revelation 1:1; Strong's Greek Lexicon, s.v. "patmos," Blue Letter Bible, www.blueletterbible.org/lexicon/g3963/kjv/tr/0-1.
11. John 10:17.
12. Matthew 7:7.
13. Romans 8:27.
14. 1 Corinthians 14:2.
15. 1 Corinthians 13:1.
16. Acts 2:8.
17. Romans 8:16.
18. 1 Corinthians 12:7–11.
19. 1 Corinthians 14:1.
20. John 20:21.
21. Revelation 22:13.

Acknowledgments

1. Ecclesiastes 4:9.

ABOUT THE AUTHOR

STEPHANIE IKE OKAFOR is a dynamic leader, executive pastor, and podcast host, as well as the author of *Moving Forward: Biblical Teachings for Walking in Purpose*. She is the co-creator and co-host of the podcast series *The Same Room*, and she pastors a vibrant faith community in Hollywood at ONE Church under the leadership of pastors Touré Roberts and Sarah Jakes Roberts. After an encounter with God at the age of nine, Stephanie Ike Okafor developed a desire to spread the gospel. She is committed to helping people seek after Jesus, know that He's real, and discover their identity in Him.

ABOUT THE TYPE

This book was set in Celeste, a typeface that its designer, Chris Burke (b. 1967), classifies as a modern humanistic typeface. Celeste was influenced by Bodoni and Waldman, but the strokeweight contrast is less pronounced. The serifs tend toward the triangular, and the italics harmonize well with the roman in tone and width. It is a robust and readable text face that is less stark and modular than many of the modern fonts, and has many of the friendlier old-face features.